Women Claim Islam

Women Claim Islam

Creating Islamic Feminism
through Literature

MIRIAM COOKE

Routledge • New York • London

Published in 2001 by
Routledge
29 West 35th Street
New York, NY 10001

Published in Great Britain by
Routledge
11 New Fetter Lane
London EC4P 4EE

Copyright © 2001 by Routledge
Routledge is an imprint of the Taylor & Francis Group.

Printed in the United States of America on acid-free paper.

10 9 8 7 6 5 4 3 2 1

LIBRARY OF CONGRESS CATALOGING-IN-PUBLICATION DATA

Cooke, Miriam.
Women claim Islam : creating Islamic feminism through literature /
Miriam Cooke.
p. cm.
ISBN 0-415-92553-3 — ISBN 0-415-92554-1 (pbk.)
1. Muslim women—Arab countries—History—20th century. 2. Muslim
women—Arab countries—Intellectual life—20th century. 3. Feminism—Arab
countries—History—20th century. 4. Feminism in literature. I. Title.

HQ1170 .C752000

00-035315

Contents

Introduction

In 1975 the United Nations launched its Decade for Women (1975–85). Responding to women's local and international networking activities, it drew new attention to women and to their changing roles, responsibilities, and status in the world. The Decade focused concern on the many forms of injustice that women endure, but it also celebrated the fact that women have become increasingly powerful and visible as they intervene in global politics. Women's unprecedented independence as a result of the revolution in reproduction technology and their massive entry into the paid workforce has begun to erode the patriarchal system. Women acting with women on behalf of women are turning to alternative communities where their identities and roles will not be fixed and subordinated.

Arab women, historically invisible, are part of this trend. Arab women whose education and mobility allow them to see and project themselves as public intellectuals are becoming visibile at the local, national, and international levels. It is, of course, possible that this fin-de-siècle moment may be no different from those that preceded it, that like their foremothers these Arab women may not enter history. Yet there is a possibility that this time they may be remembered, because they are not alone either at home or in the world.

Protesting their many exclusions from their nations' narratives, Arab women writers are demanding to be heard and seen. They have been left out of history, out of the War Story, out of narratives of emigration and exile, out of the physical and hermeneutical spaces of religion. There are several reasons for the recent proliferation of Arab women's voices, but the most compelling are the recent dominance in many Arab countries of Islamic discourse, which gives unprecedented importance to women, and the revolution in information technology, which is enabling a new kind of networking that links local, national, and transnational players and is instrumental in fomenting a global conception of identity and community.

At the threshold of the third millennium, religious groups everywhere are becoming more vocal and visible, and they are placing women at the symbolic center of their concerns and debates. They are posing tough questions about women's new roles and responsibilities in the information age, and these questions are shaping the debate about how economic, social, and political survival can be managed without sacrificing traditional, religiously sanctioned norms. While conservative religious authorities in the Arab world are publishing tomes about women's importance to the virtuous Muslim community, they are also dictating constricting rules for women's appropriate behavior. As more and more Muslim women realize that this official preoccupation with women's bodies threatens their ability to make their own decisions, they are doing something about it. Some reject the term "feminist" to describe what they are doing. Some act as feminists even if they do not use the term. A few are happy to call themselves feminists.

In *Women Claim Islam,* I use "feminist" to refer to women who think and do something about changing expectations for women's social roles and responsibilities. Why do I do so, despite widespread resistance to the term as connoting Western women's activism and radical political movements? Throughout the twentieth century, women in the Arab world have tried to find alternative terminology. However, whether they name themselves *unthawiyat, nassawiyat* (Al-Ali 1997: 174), "womanists" (Zuhur 1993: 32), or "remakers of women" (Abu Lughod 1998: 5–6), these educated, privileged, and engaged women are all struggling to improve the situation for women. While I too have tried to find synonyms for the word "feminism," I found myself compelled to define the synonym in such a way that it would serve the same function as "feminism." And so I use the word without apologies. I do so because I do not believe that its meaning should be restricted to a narrow notion of public action, nor do I accept the judgment that it is a culturally specific term. I want to keep the word because I believe in the power of naming, and feminism is a powerful name with historical resonance. Should I give in to pressure from several quarters and reject the term that describes their labors as imperialist? I am convinced that I will help to erase, in the words of the cultural critic Anne McClintock, "the long histories of women's resistance to local and imperialist patriarchies. . . . If all feminisms are derided as a pathology of the West, there is a very real danger that Western, white feminists will remain hegemonic, for the simple reason that such women have comparatively privileged access to publishing, the international media, education and money" (1995: 384).

Feminism is much more than an ideology driving organized political movements. It is, above all, an epistemology. It is an attitude, a frame of mind that highlights the role of gender in understanding the organization of society. Feminism provides analytical tools for assessing how expectations for men's and women's behavior have led to unjust situations, particularly but not necessarily only for women. Feminism seeks justice wherever it can find it. Feminism involves political and intellectual awareness of gender discrimination, a rejection of behaviors furthering such discrimination, and the advocacy of activist projects to end discrimination and to open opportunities for women to participate in public life. While clearly connected, awareness, rejection, and activism are not progressive stages that culminate in their totality. In other words, the activist has not necessarily first understood how the situation she is working to change has been damaging to women. She may never have said no to anyone before she joined a movement. Activism might precede awareness, or operate independently of it. So might rejection. Awareness might never develop beyond itself, rejection might never be informed by a specific agenda. Activism, too, might never pass through the negativity of rejection. A woman or group of women might remain positively focused on constructing new systems without ever having said no to the old system. This definition of feminism describes changing states of consciousness, each reflecting women's understanding of themselves and their situations as related to their social and biological condition. Thus defined, feminism is not bound to one culture. It is no more Arab than it is American, no more Mediterranean than it is North European. It is this definition of feminism that I am using in this book.

Women Claim Islam examines how women are reimagining foundational narratives: from historiography to the War Story to narratives of migration to the most recent engagement in Islamic discourse. I focus on Arab women's autobiographies and novels because it is there that one can most clearly see the individual creating alternative realities. Alternative does not mean separate or irrelevant. These reflections on personal experience and forays into fiction may provide the blueprints for the future.

Perhaps no historical event of this century has affected Muslim women more than Ayatollah Khomeini's 1979 Islamic revolution in Iran. It marked the first victory of a religiously inspired political movement to establish a theocracy in modern times. Islam came to be viewed as an instrument for bringing a subalternized people into representation and potential hegemony. It was regarded with suspicion by secular states with Muslim majorities and also by Western nation-states with ambitions in Muslim-dominated regions. Draining individual Muslims out of their representations, except as religious fanatics or terrorists, the Western media began to represent Islam as threatening. Arab regimes, whether Tunisian, Moroccan, or Syrian, also reacted to the manifestations of local activism by outlawing nascent Islamist movements. Beyond its obviously militaristic dimension, Islamic global prominence has assumed a special guise: women as embodiments of this newly powerful religion, or as cultural symbols demarcating public and private spaces.

The Islamic revolution has highlighted women both as objects and as subjects. Iranian women's mobilization on behalf of the anti-shah, anti-West revolution put the question of women, politics, and religion on the international agenda. As is now well-known, nationalist women, most of them recently and expediently veiled, supported the clerics in their resistance against the westernized shah. They had adopted the veil, which confounded political and religious symbolism, to demonstrate their anti-West nationalist convictions. They were eager to veil because they believed that to wear this symbol of nationalist mobilization against the westernized shah would demonstrate their commitment and importance to the nationalist movement and speed the advent of a new pro-women era. They were not, however, prepared for its legal imposition. When the revolutionary clerics came to power, the veil became a compulsory uniform representing women's piety, but also, importantly, the country's religiosity. The nationalist choice thus became a religious mandate. Nor has this been an isolated phenomenon. During the twenty years following the revolution in Iran, religious extremists everywhere have stressed the role of women in their ideologies and plans of campaign. Newly pious men have arrogated to themselves the right to monitor women's appearance and behavior. Looked at from afar and often through the lens of a television camera, it seems that women have no choice but to obey. The stories we hear from Afghanistan, Sudan, and Algeria as well as from conservative religious communities in Israel and the United States tell of women changing their dress and being content to remain in a home that has been symbolically transformed into the "nation" of this new community.

While some women are disempowered, others have been galvanized by these developments. Some are responding to the silencing conditions inherent in their newly globalized situation even though they know that to speak out risks charges of cultural betrayal. By relocating their words from a local to a global context, they are negotiating new transnational realities that cut across local and familial identifications. What do they mean when they sometimes repeat what the men say about women's roles as subservient upholders of cultural values? It is important to note that acquiescence with traditional gender roles and behavioral expectations at one moment does not necessarily contradict resistance at another—and sometimes even the same— moment. Drawing on the symbolic capital provided by the Qur'an and Traditions, or the authenticated sayings and deeds of the Prophet Muhammad that form the basis of Islamic law, some Muslim Arab feminists are examining the gendered formation of Islamic epistemology. They do not question the sacrality of the Qur'an, but they do examine the temporality of its interpretations.

Women public intellectuals in postrevolutionary Iran provide a powerful instance of gender activism within an Islamic framework. In 1992 a group of women founded *Zanan*, an Islamic and explicitly feminist journal. Reading the Qur'an from a women's viewpoint, the contributors aim not merely to produce new legal interpretations for a small group of religious scholars, but rather to "awaken women so that they will proclaim their rights" and thus transform society (Najmabadi 1998: 72, 66, 71). Like nineteenth-century American Protestant women reformers, they are appropriating "religious authority and social power [using] religious authority as both guide and shield in their efforts to claim the right to shape public reality" (Buchanan 1996: 141). By juxtaposing religious texts of all sorts with Western feminist writings they are confusing the "comforting categories of Islamic and secular [and are making] West and East speak in a new combined tongue in dialogue with rather than as negating of each other." Afsaneh Najmabadi claims that their radical interpretations are reconfiguring space in such a way that "women of different outlooks can have a common stake" (Najmabadi 1998: 77). These Iranian women have chosen the most public of venues to demand a hearing so as to enter spaces previously closed to them.

Like their Iranian sisters, Arab women who situate themselves within an overtly religious discourse as "Islamic feminists" (see chapter 3 for a definition of the term), are objecting to the fact that women have been excluded from the physical and discursive spaces of Islam. Egyptian-American historian Leila Ahmed goes so far as to posit the evolution of two Islams, one for women and another for men. Women, who were generally illiterate, visited the mosques for private, personal reasons only. They did not attend the Friday congregational prayer where men heard "the official [male, of course] orthodox interpretations of religion . . . telling them week by week and month by month what it meant to be a Muslim" (Ahmed 1999: 123–24). Women worked out their own understandings of Islam, paying "little or no attention to the utterances and exhortations of sheikhs or any sort of official figures." The Islam of women, overwhelmingly oral and aural, "stresses moral conduct and emphasizes Islam as a broad

ethos and ethical code and as a way of understanding and reflecting on the meaning of one's life and of human life more generally" (126). Islam, however, is not gender-specific but rather a
faith system and way of life open equally to women and men.

Women's protest against male hegemony in the production of
official Islamic knowledge is not new. Already at the end of the
nineteenth century, women like the Lebanese Zaynab al-Fawwaz
were framing feminist demands and arguments within Islamic
norms and values in order to deflect criticism that their inspira-
tions and goals were Western. By the 1920s, feminism as a discourse and a practice was becoming visible in Egypt and
Lebanon, with secular and observant men and women debating
the extent to which Muslim scripture and law allowed women to
participate with men in the public domain.

A very hot topic at the time was the question of the veil and its
divine ordination. In 1923, Huda Shaarawi, the founder and president of the Egyptian Feminist Union, had staged a public
demonstration in the Cairo railway station by taking off her veil
in front of a crowd. Much ink had been spilled on the topic of
unveiling, but after this momentous event, the issue gained reality
and substance as committed Muslim women added their voices to
the debate. The Lebanese Nazira Zayn al-Din (1908–1976),
daughter of a Muslim authority, complains in her *Unveiling and
Veiling* (1928) that Muslim prescriptions for women, particularly
concerning the veil, have been historically framed by men. She
devotes hundreds of pages to a passionate, well-documented refu-
tation of the Islamic scholars' insistence that veiling is religiously
binding. The international reaction to the book was so heated
and immediate that the young Nazira published *The Girl and the
Shaykhs* (1929). It is a collection of dozens of the reviews, particularly those by the shaykhs of the title, as well as her own
responses. Far from being cowed by those who wanted to silence
her, she is galvanized. She emphasizes that women "are more
worthy of interpreting verses that have to do with women's duties

and rights than men, for they are the ones that are directly addressed" (Zayn al-Din 1998b; 82). She reiterates her right as a good Muslim woman, daughter of a good Muslim father—a self-identification that peppers the prose—to investigate her religion and culture without constraint. It is blind imitation of tradition as well as foreigners, she writes, that contradicts the spirit of the Qur'an and that has led Muslims to their current sorry plight (110–14). Anticipating the Islamic feminist discourse of the latter part of the century, she insists that Islamic law is about each Muslim's unmediated relationship with God, rather than a manual to police individual behavior and human interactions. In 1998 the Syrian critic Bouthaina Shaaban edited and reissued these texts, which had fallen out of circulation during the intervening seventy years (Zayn al-Din 1998a, 15, 32).

The reappearance of these radical documents in the late 1990s underscores a growing trend: Muslim women are demanding equal access to scriptural truth at a time when Islamic discourse is on the rise. Since the late 1970s and the Iranian revolution, popular preachers throughout the Muslim world have become increasingly influential. The mass sale of cassette sermons has become a powerful way of disseminating Islamic ideas and language among all classes. Indeed, the popularity of this Islamic discourse at all levels of society has wrought a change in the conception of the public sphere. It is no longer only the religious experts who know and use the special idiom of Islamic discourse and disputation. Attentive listening to these tapes educates those who would not otherwise have access to the concepts and the terminology. Even the uneducated are becoming empowered to debate religion in public.

Until recently it was men whose sermons were taped, but during the 1990s women preachers have gained access to the mosques and their sermons are beginning to circulate, even if not commercially but rather by word of mouth or by personal tapes. In contrast with the findings of many students of Islamic fundamentalism that indicate that the majority of participants come from the lower middle classes (see Lawrence 1989), the recent wave of Islamization seems to be having an impact on all classes. Samia Serageldin researched the new religious practices of upper-class women in Cairo during the 1990s. In December 1999 field notes that she shared with me, she wrote that middle-aged women brought up in secular homes are networking around Islamic practices, such as "lessons, which are given on specific days of the week in a specific mosque by specific women who have studied formally for at least two years and have received a certificate to 'preach' by the Azhar or other authorities. These classes, although they are held in a mosque or *zawiya* [religious space], are in fact by invitation or referral only." One of the best-known of the preachers is Miss Sawsan, a former English teacher who speaks weekly to hundreds of women seated uncomfortably on the floor. Topics covered span the gamut from correct preparation for prayer to headcovering. A more focused topic is *tagwid*, or the correct reading and pronunciation of the Qur'an. During Ramadan these practices intensify and new ones are added. The *tarawih*, or optional prayers after the breaking of the fast, bring women and men together in the mosques on a daily basis throughout the month. Serageldin points out ironically that time tends to be made for these *tarawih* prayers despite these women's "gruelling social schedules—one must remember that all this has to fit in between organizing the Hanae Mori fashion show for the charity benefit gala of the Rotary Club, attending the Aida opera at the Pyramids, etc." (e-message from Serageldin 12/23/1999).

In Saudi Arabia, women interpreters of the Qur'an have become prominent in the last two years, and they are appealing to women of all classes also. On Mondays in downtown Jeddah, Samira Jamjum lectures to a hall full of women. On Saturdays, it is the turn of the acclaimed religious authority Dr. Fatima Umar Naseef to lecture to over five hundred women. Her clarion cry is taken straight from the Prophet Muhammad: "Seek knowledge wherever you can find it, even in China." She has devoted an entire chapter of her *Women in Islam* to a woman's right to seek knowledge and to "learn about her rights and duties and to put this knowledge into practice" (Naseef 1999: 81).

Dr. Fatima, as she is known, is having an impact on women of all ages. Young women told me, their eyes shining, that Dr. Fatima made them see that the Qur'an was addressing each one of them directly. Older women praised her for her ability to give them scriptural tools to justify their behavior and aspirations for full participation in their country's future. In the past two years, Saudi Arabia has been experiencing the full blast of the information technology revolution: satellite dishes dot the city skylines, unmonitored cellular phones interrupt meetings and conversations, and, since March of 1999, access to the Internet from Saudi domains was finally approved. A window of opportunity for a social movement seems to be cracking open.

On the last day of a ten-day visit to Saudi Arabia in November 1999, I was granted an interview with Dr. Fatima. I had heard from everyone about her unprecedented charismatic public talks and television appearances, and I wanted to know whether Dr. Fatima felt that the information revolution was going to change local and national norms.

"Women here have always been networked, always able to be in touch with whomever they wanted, even when alone at home," she explained. "Anyhow, you have the same phenomenon in the U.S. today. I have read that millions of Americans are now working out of their own homes, whether by choice or by necessity. They are not together but they are also not isolated. Like women here, they are even more connected than ever before. They have actually chosen physical isolation so as to be able to enhance their virtual community."

A historically minded person might challenge such a comparison between a forced physical isolation and one that is chosen. A cultural critic might agree with Dr. Fatima. In a postmodern world, history is flattened so that synchronic, cross-cultural similarities can be identified without recourse to diachronic differences. In other words, it matters less when and how a particular configuration of human relationships was achieved than how it actually functions. Global interconnection and cultural intertwinement are becoming the norm. Even in the most conservative, sex-segregated society, women are now able to communicate transnationally and to exchange new understandings of religious and social norms and values.

Whereas before it was only religious scholars and religious-minded intellectuals who negotiated the parameters of what is and is not permissible, today men and women from all walks of life are recognizing that the terms of local debates about present practice and future directions are being Islamized and that if they wish to be heard they must learn Islam's rules. Pakistani sociologist Farida Shaheed describes a growing perception that despite the wide diversity of the Muslim world, "the cultural articulation of patriarchy (through structures, social mores, laws and political power) is increasingly justified by reference to Islam and Islamic doctrine" (Shaheed 1995: 79). Moroccan sociologist and writer Fatima Mernissi goes further. She describes Islamist groups' growing obsession with women's bodies and social roles during the 1980s. She sees their high profile as "a veritable media campaign." She is alarmed by recent republications, widely and cheaply available, of thirteenth- through nineteenth-century texts by misogynist Islamic scholars (Mernissi 1991: 97–99).

Islamic discourse has so pervaded the public and private spheres that those who wish to remain a part of public discourse need to know how to use it. Abdullahi an-Na'im, a Sudanese scholar of Islamic law, has written that "the advocates of the human rights of women should realize that they have no alternative but to engage in an Islamic discourse. Whatever they may think of it, the fact of the matter is that Islamic groups have already succeeded in 'Islamizing' the terms of reference of public discourse in most Islamic societies" (an-Na'im 1995: 59). Women are asking how new technologies and the cultures and values they entail will be adapted to a well-understood notion of the Qur'an and the Sunna as eternal. How can one be modern, global, and yet observant? What role will Islam play in shaping ethical, modern citizens who are able to survive in, as well as to critique, a rapidly transforming world? Will Islamically inspired responses to globalization help or harm women? How will horizontal networking transform human relationships that have traditionally been based on vertical hierarchies?

Networking can create collective identities of resistance to many forces, above all to globalization. These resistant communities may arise out of exclusion from the global system, but they do not necessarily eschew its instrumentalities. Societies that could not modernize in a world that valued industrialization, and the physical and engineering transformations it required, are now able to imagine a way of connecting on an equal footing with those who were previously unreachable competitors. Where value is gauged according to the scale of integration into the world system—for example, through market flows and linked production—there are unprecedented opportunities, as well as unprecedented risks of failure and terminal exclusion.

Globalization has collapsed local colonial legacies, postcolonial failures, and neocolonial threats into a single condition of vulnerability that demands new responses. A much-trumpeted response has been Islamization, particularly in its militant form. The lesser known, but corollary reaction has taken another form. Some people, especially those who position themselves as Islamic feminists, are inventing ways to navigate between forced changes necessary for survival, a critique of globalized modernity, and a viable means of self-projection that retains dignity, morality, and integrity. In this balancing act, women are gaining symbolic importance. Ahmed notes that Islamic authorities who had long sought to separate men's Islam from that of women are now trying to bridge the gender divide. Gender-specific religious spheres are being forced into greater proximity so as to produce a new united Islamic ethos and discourse (Ahmed 1999: 129).

Yet even as individuals and groups with Islamic feminist agendas challenge the destructive potential of globalization, they are finding ways to benefit from it. Networking with each other across the oceans and the continents by phone, fax, and the Internet, identifying themselves as belonging to a specific religious community, more and more women are engaging with and interrogating the norms and values of Islam as a cultural and religious practice and discourse. Rooted in their specific places but speaking out transnationally as part of the world Muslim community, or *umma*, they are more likely to have an impact because their interventions cannot be so easily silenced by kin or other authorities opposed to their message. How can they find this speaking position that is both local and global? In what follows, I argue that Islam provides the symbolic capital for the construction of such an apparently contradictory rhetorical space.

Religions transcend geographical boundaries. This is particularly true for Islam. Its very material connection to Arabia, where it found its beginnings, provides unusual possibilities for constructing a territorialized transcultural identity with a virtual center and a virtual diaspora. Historically, religions have played a key role in determining identity at both the national and the transnational levels. Some scholars, like the French historian Fernand Braudel, have argued that before the rise of nationalism in the nineteenth century, "peoples felt truly united only by the bonds of religious belief, in other words by civilization" (Braudel 1995: 824). Culture and civilization were in some sense one with religion. Religion often assumed primary importance in indigenous self-identification as civic rights came to be associated with religion. Consider Iran. Before the Constitutional

Revolution of 1905–11, the country was called the "Shiite nation," and only afterward the "Iranian nation." The new definition of the nation "as a people of diverse languages and religions all equal before the law challenged the most basic hierarchy of *millat* [nation] as conceptualized by Islam" (Tavakoli-Targhi 1990: 93, 99). In the Maghreb, the colonized Muslim and Jewish communities assumed the characteristics of national cultures. Jacques Derrida writes that they were *musulmans* or *juifs indigènes* first, and then citizens of their geographic location (see chapter 2). The Moroccan writer Tahar Benjelloun claims that whereas Algerian Christians were considered French, and the Jews became French after 1870, the Muslims had no nationality beyond "indigenous," a term referring "to those placed at the bottom of the social ladder. Indigenous=inferior" (Benjelloun 1998: 53).

Religion conferred or denied civic rights. A transnational identification became an ethnocultural affiliation that coincided with geography and history. In other words, religion was the key element in indigenous identity (Derrida 1996: 34–35, 66, 68). In the postcolonial period, the memory of identity in places like Tunisia, Algeria, and Morocco is of belonging to a religion. Islam served as a kind of spiritual, cultural nation, which then provided the site of resistance to the West. This was the rhetoric during the fight for independence, and it is the rhetoric today, even in places as secular and westernized as Turkey, where "Islam appears as mortar in a new nationalism that functions in opposition to Kemalism which aims to be independent of the local patterns embodied in the Islamic religion" (Gole 1996: 139). This new Turkish nationalism rejects the westernization that marked the secular regime of Kemal Ataturk and replaces it with a place-based attention to a historical, religious, now national identity.

Religions can also be used ahistorically to construct transnational identities within virtual communities, committed to values that transcend time and space. Yet even as the community is free of geography it may *at the same time* be able to invoke it. That political entities have sought and gained secular power in the name of a particular god does not mean that their physical power base became the nation of that religion. Yet that was often how it appeared because the sacred label justified assuming power across social, economic, political, geographic, and cultural boundaries. It allowed some religious rulers to invent their national history along religious lines and then to name their region a confessional nation.

Islam provides the symbolic capital otherwise unavailable to today's new nations. In contrast with nationalist claims for "pure blood," which critics reject as spurious, Muslims can invoke and indeed do have easy access to the pure origins of the Islamic nation. No matter how contaminated by foreign domination, Muslims seeking an unadulterated past have the scriptures as recourse. Islam as a religion may evolve and change as interpretations of its texts proliferate, but the sources of these interpretations remain intact. The Muslim nation may become an expedient invention whose obliteration is safe from the anxiety produced by territoriality. When new geographical borders are drawn, Muslim communities may find themselves politically split. Yet they retain cultural and symbolic links with coreligionists through a transnational imaginary and modern communications. At home in the borderzones that have assured them actual and cultural survival, they are comparable with today's migrants and refugees. They have not *become* migrants moving constantly across and within national borders. Rather, it is their geographically flexible identity, which oscillates between diaspora and origin, that characterizes Muslim identity.

As members of a world community, Muslims can think transnationally while retaining deep connections with a specific place, whether it be of birth, of choice, or of compulsion. From Islam's beginnings in seventh century Arabia and spreading quickly east to China and west to Spain, the Islamic oikumene formed the primary site of belonging for Muslims. The Muslim world has always functioned as a vast network linked by urban nodes where Islamic knowledge was pursued and produced. Travel and cosmopolitanism are a necessary part of all Muslims' spiritual and material identities: the *hajj*, or the annual pilgrimage to Mecca, the *hijra*, which "is the obligation to migrate from lands where the practice of Islam is constrained to those where in principle no such constraints exist. Visits to local or regional shrines (*ziyaras*) and travel in search of knowledge (*rihla*) provide further examples of religiously inspired travel." Travel, whether literal or symbolic, always anticipates return to "a mythical realm where home, the 'fixed point' of departure and return, is reimagined and further travel inspired." Travel is the *sine qua non*, of every Muslim's daily reality, and "has contributed significantly to shaping the religious imagination in both the past and the present" (Eickelman and Piscatori 1990: 5, xiii, xvi). This insistence on actual and symbolic travel allows for simultaneous self-positionings in the local and the global and then back to another local, in the present and the past and then back to a transformed present.

Muslims can draw on two different stories connecting identity with territory. The first is transnational and deterritorialized. Pointing *forward*, it narrates social fragmentation and ad hoc consociations. Muslims are scattered throughout most countries of the world; they are not members of a single nation. At least once in the lifetime of each Muslim there is awareness of this radical internationalism when the individual performs the sacred duty of pilgrimage to Mecca. During the month of the *hajj*, Muslim pilgrims from all corners of the world, grouped usually by national designation, converge on two Saudi Arabian cities. Mecca and Medina become microcosms of the multicultural Muslim world.

The second Muslim story is national. Looking *backward*, it roots itself in a specific territory. Despite the fact that they are citizens of most countries of the world, Muslims can invoke the unifying politics of *umma*, known in the modern period as pan-Islamism. In so doing, they link the transnational with individual national stories by projecting themselves as the diaspora of a seventh-century bedouin tribe in the Arabian Peninsula. This diaspora has been held together by its historic links with this simulacric origin. These connections are created by two of the five pillars, or basic tenets, of Islam: the *hajj*, or pilgrimage, which each Muslim is expected to undertake at least once in a lifetime; and by *salat*, or the five daily prayers in Arabic, the language of the Qur'an. Ritual travel to a site in the Arabian Peninsula and daily use of its language, as well as of a compass to orient the faithful to Mecca from wherever they might be in the world, compel a transnational consciousness that links Muslims in their specific places with the symbolic heart of their religion. Additionally, social hierarchy in the Muslim world structures the Arabia-centeredness of Muslim identity for a small number of elites. To be *sharif*, or noble in Muslim terminology, is to be able to trace virtual roots back to a single place and a single family, those of the Quraishi tribe of the Prophet Muhammad in seventh-century Arabia, regardless of where one was born or lives. Genealogy thus becomes another deterritorialized means for the elite to connect to place of origin.

Placed within this context of founding community, linguistic and genealogical heritage, the *hajj* may be interpreted as something other than the exceptional gathering of different races, ethnicities, and cultures in two Arabian cities. It can be seen rather as an occasion when Indonesians, Americans, and Senegalese join their Arab "cousins" to make the sentimental journey "home" to Mecca, a return they anticipate five times a day when they orient themselves for prayer.

At the end of the twentieth century, women are using these two Muslim stories to situate themselves transnationally as strong women and righteous Muslims committed to social justice. At the same time, they root themselves in the territory of Islam to demand authority to speak out against those who are trying to exalt them as symbols but to exclude them as persons.

Women Claim Islam traces through the literary history of Arab women from the nineteenth century to the present when more and more women are interpellating authorities, above all religious authorities. What interests me always is not the individual genius but women's literary communities. Only by concentrating on their collective cultural production can we see that Arab women intellectuals are everywhere challenging metanarratives that write them out of active political presence. Their questioning reveals that official histories are at best partial, shedding light on one aspect of reality only, the male sector, thereby distorting what actually happened and limiting the possibilities for what might happen in the future.

The two stories that I question in chapter 1 are what I have called the War Story (Cooke 1997) and the success in diaspora story. First, I compare the Gulf War texts of Kuwaiti and Iraqi women with two versions of the War Story, one by U.S. secretary of defense Richard Cheney and the other by Iraqi president Saddam Hussein. Many military technologies have come and gone, and yet the ancient frame narrative of the War Story remains intact. Even the Gulf War that seemed to undermine the binaries thought proper to the experience of war was quickly rearticulated in terms of familiar oppositions. The process involved the invocation of unstable notions like the "line in the sand," which paradoxically reassured viewers about the conventionality of this cyberwar. There was a front aligning the good guys against the bad guys. These versions erase the reality of the war that saw women in combat and Iraqi civilians as targets. Second, I turn to women's versions of life in the diaspora that undermine triumphalist justifications for departure from the homeland. The truth of the matter is that many emigrants, even those who are educated, find themselves doing menial work in their new homes. Eking out the most miserable of lives, they keep their failure a secret, and so the process goes on repeating itself. The question then is: How to break the cycle? The Lebanese Emily Nasrallah writes about societies that expect their children to find success only outside the country. Her stories reveal how flawed a system is that encourages the best and brightest to leave without any guarantee of success. Visits to or from emigrants, particularly women, reveal that both communities are damaged when diaspora is preferred over remaining in the homeland.

Chapter 2 examines the role of the mother tongue in women's and men's construction of identity. Comparing autobiographical texts by four colonial and postcolonial North African writers—Assia Djebar, Abdelkebir Khatibi, Albert Memmi, and Jacques Derrida—I conclude that the mother tongue is a site of power and threat because of its associations with mothers' and women's strength. The degree to which the individual can use it positively depends on gender, coloniality, and religion. Whereas the men wrestle with this first language, and especially with its problematic associations with their mothers, Djebar lovingly engages it. She describes her mother tongue, the Berber women's *Ursprache*, as the key to unlocking what lies behind the gaps and silences that surround women's creative contributions to history. Strategically essentializing women's language, Djebar finds the tools with which to deconstruct the master's house. By splitting language and birth from identity, these writers are installing doubt at the heart of the unified autonomous self, and demonstrating how constructed are all conceptions of fixed identity.

In chapters 3 and 4 I analyze several texts that I characterize as Islamic feminist. What does Islamic feminism mean? Is it not a contradiction? What is the difference between the ascribed identity of "Muslim" and the achieved identity of "Islamic"? When do women who think of themselves as Muslims, or whom others describe as Muslim because that is the religion of their birth and of their identity cards, become Islamic? Reading literary texts of two Maghrebi women, Assia Djebar (b. 1938) and Fatima Mernissi (b. 1941), and two Egyptian women, Nawal El Saadawi (b. 1931) and Zaynab al-Ghazali (b. 1917), I argue that Islamic feminism is not an identity but rather one of many possible speaking positions. I have deliberately chosen women whose credentials as either Islamic or feminist are open to question by purists on both sides. El Saadawi is clearly a feminist, but Islamic?! Zaynab al-Ghazali is a self-declared Islamist, but a feminist?! By focusing on utterly different works and writers I hope to test how the identification of Islamic feminism works. These writers are insisting on women's right to claim a place in the annals of their people. They describe the Prophet Muhammad as the leader of a feminist revolution that was almost immediately betrayed. They tell stories that expose current corruption and create possibilities for imagining alternative futures. They criticize the ways in which Muslim authorities prevent them from doing what they want, even as they uphold those aspects of their culture that align them with their Muslim sisters and brothers against threatening outsiders.

In chapter 5 I trace how those who position themselves as Islamic feminists share a rhetorical stance that I call "multiple critique." Although few are Islamists, they are profiting from the changes happening within the most conservative sectors of their societies. Reorientation of loyalties at the local level has allowed them to imagine new associations and create new networks. They are drawing on the symbolic capital of Islam to construct a multiple critique, one instrumental in imagining speaking positions that facilitate intervention in the production of new situated knowledges. Multiple critique provides women with the basis for power in Muslim communities. It enables them to emerge into representation from the margins. As they seek a religiously sanctioned openness to women's public agency, they foreground the tension between eternity and history, between the divine and the human, between domestic and national and even transnational spheres. They are careful not to cast them as mutually exclusive contradictions. In each case, cross-cultural images play a defining role. At a time when our lives are being hypervisualized, when the influence of the image is often greater than that of the written text, the physical, cultural, and visual baggage we bring to conversations with others carries heavy weight. The challenge is to break through the cellophane of images with which Arabs and Americans cover each other. So as to remain open to transformation by the process of mutual engagement.

Chapter 6 reviews recent developments in the academic study of Arab Muslim women in the United States. During the late 1980s, Arab-American women began to take responsibility for the production of knowledge about women, gender, and religion in the Arab world. Even though many would check "white" on a census form, the politicization of their identity in the wake of the Gulf War has led some to call themselves women of color. This new self-projection affirms their locatedness in the United States and links them with other minoritarian groups within the United States in a politics of resistance. From this perspective they are adding new voices and perspectives on what is happening to women in the Arab world. As a result of their intellectual interventions, the study of Arab Muslim women has become an important site for the transformation of cross-cultural images.

Writing this book has taught me how problematic is the notion of a single, unified identity, whether ascribed or achieved. Examining Arab women's rhetorical strategies has shown me how we *all* belong to multiple communities simultaneously. This multiple belonging does not lead to a pathological condition. We are not all suffering from multiple personality disorders. At each instant we recognize ourselves as identical with some and different from others. Those with whom we identify at some point may allow us a platform from which to speak. Sometimes not.

Identity is constantly constructed and projected in the stories we tell. Narratives put order and shape into the chaos of our lives. We need to remain conscious of this ordering mechanism in ourselves but also in others. The story I tell about myself here is only one of many that I could have dreamed up out of my multiple identifications. At a time when large numbers of people are on the move around the globe and communicating instantly with each other wherever they may be, notions of stable identity based on geography, language, or race are falling apart. It is not, however, enough to say that we are living in a time beyond identity; we have to understand what it means to be always dynamically, but also seamlessly fragmented. In *Women Claim Islam*, I explore the ways in which Arab women intellectuals navigate among and through multiple identifications, with a common purpose of projecting their voices as public intellectuals calling for justice and freedom.

1

Arab Women's Literary History

Before looking at the most recent developments in Arab women's writings, which have moved from a generally secular focus to an increasingly Islamic orientation, it is necessary to situate these writings more broadly within their historical context. In this chapter I examine the ways in which some Arab women have used their stories to change conceptions of modern Arabic literature. There are many issues that have concerned Arab writers in the twentieth century, but two narratives have had a particular impact on the way in which Arab intellectuals shape their experience. The first is the War Story; the second is the story about the emigrant's experience after leaving the homeland.

It is not generally known that Arab women have been writing and publishing fiction since the end of the nineteenth century. Three Lebanese women, Zaynab Fawwaz (1860–1914), Labiba Hashim (1880–1947), and Mayy Ziyada (1886–1941), and in Egypt Aisha Taimuriyya (1840–1902), should be considered the pioneers of Arab women's literary history. The first half of the twentieth century witnessed more women taking up the pen, yet their works received so little notice that it was as though they had not written. It was only in the 1960s and 1970s that sporadic critical attention was paid to a few, like the Egyptian Nawal El Saadawi, the Lebanese Layla Baalbaki, and the Syrian Colette Khuri. During the 1980s, however, this situation changed as these women's fiction began to be translated. In 1986, at the first International Feminist Bookfair in London, two Arab women writers were introduced to the English-speaking world. The publishing house Quartet brought out in English the Lebanese Hanan al-Shaykh's controversial novel on the Lebanese civil war, *The Story of Zahra* (1980), and the Egyptian Alifa Rifaat's *Distant View of a Minaret* (1986), a collection of stories about lonely women in Cairo. Fourteen years later, Arab women writers are much better known at home and abroad.

Critical Response

Recognition abroad is more than paralleled by an upsurge in creativity at home. Even in Saudi Arabia, where women's education was introduced in the 1960s only, women are publishing in growing numbers. In November 1999 I was invited to give the keynote address to the first conference of Saudi women writers. Drawing only from cities on the Red Sea coast, the conference nonetheless managed to assemble over sixty women. The critical response to this literary activity always takes time.

The first serious attempt to categorize and take stock of the productivity of Arab women writers came in 1986, when Joseph Zeidan published a bibliography of 486 women who wrote in Arabic between the 1880s and 1980s. Almost half of these women had published two or more books. Whereas during the first half of this century there were few women writing anywhere outside the literary centers of Cairo and Beirut, by the 1970s in every single Arab country women were beginning to write. Zeidan's staging of this process is revealing. Between the late nineteenth century and 1930, he found only twenty women who had written (some in magazines only), with about five women writing per decade. This number then doubled to ten between 1930 and 1940, and during the next decade fifteen women published. Between 1950 and 1960 their numbers more than doubled to thirty-three, and between 1960 and 1970 this last number almost tripled to ninety-six. By the next decade, the last to be covered by the bibliography, 129 women were writing, even in the countries of the Arabian Peninsula where education for women was new. In 1999 Zeidan published a revised version of the 1986 bibliography to extend it up to 1996. This updated bibliography contains information on an astounding 1,271 women. In other words, with the addition of only a few years at both ends he was able to almost triple the number of entries.

Over the past century, hundreds of women have been writing despite a meager critical response. Until recently, the few scholars who were at all interested framed Arab women's writings chronologically within totalizable stages each with its own sense of closure. In general, critics have noted development from personal preoccupations to sporadic expressions of political awareness as the writers' countries went through wars of independence from colonial rule. Some critics have praised evolution from the poor to the good; from imitation through identity formation to nationalist preoccupations; from the personal to the political. Modernization is good, and particularly for women (cf. Zeidan 1995).

A closer look at the texts, however, reveals that different things were happening in different places during a single time period; women's preoccupations fluctuated from one period to another, from one country to another, and even from one woman to another at various points during her life. Individual women writers might range across a spectrum of topics, so that sometimes they might write of themselves, at other times of what was happening to the men and women in their communities. Women, like men, think and write about more than one thing at the same time, and this is particularly true in the course of a career.

Women in the Arab world have long written about politics, if often indirectly, in ways that have been particularly revealing. Their literary negotiations with those in positions of domestic, local, and international power have highlighted the tensions that postcolonial societies confront as they deal with the legacies of colonialism while trying to find an honorable place in an unfriendly world. Each novel or short story rarely serves as an allegory but rather as a stone in a mosaic where its preoccupations resonate with those of others.

Arab women respond to each other, test local possibilities, plug into transcultural concerns. Their collective literary project can best be appreciated in anthologies, which provide the context that gives the individual piece of writing meaning and impact beyond itself. Anthologies of women's writings do more than contextualize; they ensure that the collective expression is not silenced with the elimination of one voice. Anthologies exemplify the Woolfian maxim that great works and writers do not emerge out of a void but rather out of a larger literary enterprise. When Yusuf al-Sharuni published *The Night After the 1001 Nights* in 1975, he introduced twenty Egyptian women writers into a literary world that had refused to acknowledge that

women had been writing, except as oddities to be exceptional-
ized. His first words are, "Women's relationship with storytelling
is ancient," and he predictably, in view of the title of his book,
mentions Sheherezade, the legendary storyteller of *1001 Nights*.
But he is not merely drawing on myth and folklore when he
extols women's contributions to Arabic literature. He compares
literary developments in the twentieth-century Arab world,
which he calls "a radical transformation as astounding as the
invention of the automobile," with socioeconomic changes in
women's roles and rights (al-Sharuni 1975: 8). The stories al-
Sharuni anthologizes focus on women's struggles against unfair
expectations for women's behavior. Their collection in one volume with a large bibliography demonstrated for the first time
how active women have been and for how long.

Another important anthology was Layla Muhammad Salih's
Women's Literature in the Arabian Peninsula and Gulf. Its publication in 1982 revealed that despite the lack of widespread education
in the region and general representations of radical segregation
and therefore of public invisibility and political acquiescence, several women had been writing for a long time and in ways that were
remarkably critical of their societies. Many of these women questioned the relevance of the term "women's literature," preferring
to be counted with their male colleagues. Physical apartheid
should at the very least be countered with literary integration.

My own writing, whether it takes the form of monograph or
anthology, has consistently engaged Arab women's collective
literary endeavors. *War's Other Voices* (1988) collects the testimony of women who had written about the Lebanese civil
war between 1975 and 1982. I called these women the Beirut
Decentrists in order to draw attention to them as a school of
writers who had collectively contributed as women citizen-
combatants to the literature on the war. Reading their texts
together allowed me to discern a transformation in the writers'
consciousness and self-representation. For the Beirut Decentrists

the chaos could not be described as a revolution or as a just war pitting the good against the bad. It was a bad war fought for individual gain, and it destroyed the nation on whose behalf it was said to have been waged.

In *Women and the War Story* (1997), I analyzed the production of other groups of women who wrote about the Algerian war of independence, the Palestinian reactions to Israeli occupations in 1948 and then after 1967, and the Iran-Iraq War. Reading their writings *together* revealed a difference in self-perception between women who participated in the precolonial and colonial wars as opposed to postcolonial wars. Anticolonial women fighters saw themselves as doing what the men did. Cross-dressing did not change their perception of who they were and how the roles that they might play in the postbellum society might change. Women in the postcolonial wars, on the other hand, did not even have to take up arms to see themselves as combatants. They portrayed themselves as women combatants who were fighting not as men but specifically *because they were women*, sometimes directly targeted for harm. When they named what they had done "combat," they transformed their consciousness about themselves, as well as about their society. They came to understand that nations struggling to be free need all of their citizens to fight for them. When the previously excluded became combatants they changed not only the nature of the fighting, they also began to make a dent in the armor of the War Story.

The Gulf War Story

Arab women have written a great deal about war because in many ways it has become part of many of their lives. The war may be civil as in Lebanon, anticolonial as in Algeria and all the countries that shook off colonial rule in the mid-twentieth century, or apparently conventional as was the Iran-Iraq War. Alternatively, it may be more metaphorical or spiritual even, as in the notion of

jihad, or religious struggle against the current condition of ignorance and corruption (see chapter 4). This awareness of the
prevalence of violence, both organized and random, has arguably
become a part of everyday lives. Technology has facilitated the
generalization of war in postmodernity. States have sponsored
and companies have created weapons that travel such great dis-
tances that the fiction of a place of fighting has become difficult
to sustain. If there is no front and it is not clear who are the combatants, how are we to know when the fighting has begun in such
a definitive way that it warrants the name of war? And if we do
not have clear signals about the beginning of wars, how can we
end what was never declared to have started? All of this uncer-
tainty and its concomitant uncontrol is monitored by the mass
media and then telecast into homes in the heart of New York
City, the Borneo rain forest, and the Sahara Desert.

However, there is one war-related certainty: women are
involved in postcolonial wars in a way that was never before so
clear. Women may have always been with men in war as nurses,
as camp followers, as cross-dressing soldiers, but they have not
before fought *as women*. During anticolonial wars in Asia and
Africa women were represented as guerrilla fighters, hijackers,
and organizers of local resistance movements. More recently, as
in the Palestinian popular uprising, women have fought as mothers, confronting the soldiers with their maternal bodies so as to
disable conventional means of violence. Yet even when women
do not choose to engage in combat, they may be forced into it
because their bodies are officially designated military targets for
rape or for bombs.

Arab women are telling many individual stories about their
encounters with violence, both organized and disorganized.
They are eloquent about the Gulf War, which has played such an
influential role in Arab identity construction, particularly
in the United States (see chapter 6). In 1991 the controversial,
censored Kuwaiti poet-princess Su'ad al-Sabah published an

anthology of ironic and bitter poetry on the Gulf War entitled *Will You Let Me Love My Country?* The poems delve into the spiritual crisis experienced by most Arab intellectuals, but most of all by the children, in the wake of the war. She evokes the dissonance between the rhetoric of Arab unity, learned from schoolbooks, and the fragmented, fractured reality just lived in the Gulf (al-Sabah 1991: 97). Her anger at the Iraqi government does not extend to the people. As we shall see, Kuwaiti women writers understood that the Iraqi people are not to blame. She writes: "The great Iraqi people will remain in my heart forever, for they are certainly innocent" (112).

Iraqi and Kuwaiti women questioned grand narratives about medieval dictatorships confronting modern democracies, good Muslims opposing bad Muslims. These women's different stories need to be read as testimonials, a special kind of witness that allows others to glimpse another kind of reality that challenges the absoluteness of the Gulf War Story as it has been told by those in power, whether in the United States or in Iraq.

On January 17, 1991, the Gulf War broke out. Two weeks earlier, the French cultural critic Jean Baudrillard had published in the French newspaper *Libération* the first of three articles on the war. Convinced, as many of us were at the time, that the spectacle of preparations for war might dispense with the need for actual warfare, he declared his thesis: "The Gulf War will not take place." He was shortly proven wrong when in a remarkably traditional manner George Bush declared war on Iraq's Saddam Hussein. Undaunted, Baudrillard stuck to his guns. For three long weeks, the United States and its allies mercilessly bombed the Iraqis, but the inventor of hyperreality remained skeptical, asking in his second article: "The Gulf War: is it really taking place?" What, one might ask, was he questioning? The "really" or the "place"? Apparently, he could not tell if this was a war or just the "illusion of massacre" (Baudrillard 1995: 58). On March 29, 1991, he dealt the warness of the Gulf War his coup de grace: "The

Gulf War did not take place." In this final essay, he writes that

> a war without victims does not seem like a real war but
> rather the prefiguration of an experimental, blank war, or a
> war even more inhuman because it is *without human losses.*
> No heroes on the other side either, where death was most
> often that of *sacrificed extras,* left as cover in the trenches of
> Kuwait, or civilians serving as bait and martyrs for the dirty
> war. . . . The minimal losses of the coalition pose a serious
> problem, which never arose in any earlier war. The paltry
> number of deaths may be cause for self-congratulation, but
> nothing will prevent this figure being paltry. (73)

At a time when we are all fascinated by the virtuality of our lives,
it is more than ever critical that we hold on to their materiality
also.

Was the Gulf War not a war for Baudrillard because there were
so few *Western* losses and the massacre was of Iraqi *sacrificed
extras?* I suspect that it was not a war for still another reason: it did
not provide an "alibi" for savagery (76). Unlike World War II, it
did not produce great war stories. Listen to the regret and nostalgia in the following passages: "Since this war was won in advance,
we will never know what it would have been like had it existed.
We will never know what an Iraqi taking part with a chance of
fighting would have been like. We will never know what an
American taking part with a chance of being beaten would have
been like" (61). This illusion of massacre did not pit good against
evil. It had lost its libidinal attraction: "[w]ar stripped of its pas-
sions, its phantasms, its finery, its veils, its violence, its images: war
stripped bare by its technicians even, and then reclothed by them
with all the artifices of electronics, as though with a second skin"
(64). War as a woman, or rather a robot.

Baudrillard was not alone. The Gulf War was and remains for
many in the West an event hard to frame in a story. Throughout
the fall of 1990, the U.S. press was filled with debate about

intervention in southwest Asia. After the outbreak of the air war, however, the media's patriotic hype silenced dissenting voices. What followed, behind the screen of clean weapons and surgical airstrikes, was confusion, friendly fire, and a brutality that the press did not cover. What we did hear about was "a global confrontation between humanity and bestiality, a battle between civilization and barbarism. This was a war to defend the principles of modernity and reason against the forces of darkness" (Aksoy and Robins 1992: 202).

The best version of the U.S. Gulf War Story was told by Richard Cheney, the U.S. secretary of defense. It took the form of a *Final Report of Congress: Conduct of the Persian Gulf War,* that "pursuant to Title V, Public Law 102-25 . . . discusses the conduct of hostilities in the Persian Gulf theater of operations" (xiii). In seventeen pages, the "Military Victory over Iraq" is loudly trumpeted. Like all good war stories, this one provided a blueprint for the next time around. The war in question began on January 17, when President George Bush launched the first strikes on Iraq. From August, when the U.S. buildup began, the war would not have provided such a neat model for the conduct of future wars. Restricted to the shorter period, it became a circumscribed *battle* as told by John Keegan in *The Face of Battle* (1976). This battle demonstrated how well the U.S. defense system works, since it could contend with the "fourth largest army in the world, *an army hardened in long years of combat against Iran*" (xiii, my emphasis). The war confirmed that funding to the Department of Defense must not be reduced: "If we fail to fund the training and high quality we have come to expect, we will end up with an organization that may still outwardly look like a military, but that simply will not function" (xxx). The Gulf War provided an unprecedented marketing opportunity for the Department of Defense, which could show off its "revolutionary new generation of high-technology weapons" (xviii), these wonderful weapons they were testing for the first time.

This U.S. Gulf War Story, like all war stories, promised that there would be more wars because good wars make you proud (Theweleit 1993). Pride is the single most important factor in the U.S. Gulf War Story; Cheney's parting paragraph goes as follows:

> America can be *proud* of its role in the Persian Gulf war. There were lessons to be learned and problems to be sure. But overall there was an outstanding victory. We can be *proud* of our conviction and international leadership. We can be *proud* of one of the most remarkable deployments in history. We can be *proud* of our partnership in arms with many nations. We can be *proud* of our technology and the wisdom of our leaders at all levels. But most of all we can be *proud* of those dedicated young Americans soldiers, sailors, airmen and marines who showed their skill, their commitment to what we stand for, and their bravery in the way they fought this war.

These "proud"s are followed by Cheney's *own signature*.

Throughout, Cheney waxes lyrical about the military leadership, which had been "outstanding," "unique," "exceptional," "smart," "superb," "excellent," "innovative," and that the whole operation which had succeeded through a "magnificent team effort" (xxv). Above all, these soldiers were not merely effective military personnel, they were deeply human, portraying "the best in American values." Cheney concludes melodramatically that the "world will not soon forget pictures of Iraqi soldiers kissing their captors' hands" (xxvi).

So why did the world forget those other Iraqis, the ones who were plowed into the sand? Because the U.S. government and media have modified the memory of this war in such a way that the United States and its allies have emerged clean and humane. This memory of innocence has erased the charred sculptures of horror that littered the Kuwait-Basra highway on February 25, the night of the Iraqi flight. Henry A. Giroux has described this "politics of innocence" as a U.S. invention, part of a worldwide neocolonial campaign that serves "to police and constrain the potentially subversive notions of memory and public culture" (1993: 87, 89). We were not shown the victims. What we saw was the image of American liberators borrowed from World War II films depicting American soldiers liberating the concentration camps. This insistent image should have drawn international attention to the victims, the Iraqi soldiers and civilians who were at the mercy of a ruthless dictator. What it achieved instead was the purge of U.S. war crimes, erasing the struggle over the legitimacy of the war.

Ironically, Saddam Hussein's insistent declaration of victory mirrored and complemented the U.S. government War Story. As late as January 28, in an interview in Baghdad with CNN's Peter Arnett, his words are full of bombast and confidence that America is suffering "internal defeat" and that it has "miscalculated." He talks patronizingly about the good American citizens who oppose "the hostile policy" (Bengio 1992: 174–88). On February 10 he broadcasts a speech about the need to look for victory inside "this great and immortal chapter of the time that has passed" (191). Six days before the end, he focuses on Israeli aggressions, on Arab treacheries, on the aerial bombing that exacerbates the sufferings caused by the international boycott. He ends: "Dignity, glory, and *victory* for the heroes of this path, the sons of our nation and mankind" (204). Even in retreat from Kuwait, he declares victory for his "valiant men, you fought the armies of thirty states and the capabilities of an even greater number of states which supplied them with the means of aggression and support" (212).

This is the other War Story, the one the loser tells to make it look as though he has not lost, buying time while he looks for another war that will prove that he did not lose. But did Saddam Hussein lose this war? Apparently not. On January 17, 1992, the world media reported on the parade through the streets of Baghdad held to celebrate the first anniversary of Iraq's great 1991 victory. Nor was this his last hurrah! On January 17, 1998, Saddam Hussein gave a speech in honor of the seventh anniversary of the start of Gulf War II. Describing himself as "the fearless defender of the Arabs and all poor nations against the American tyrant," he declared himself ready to launch a jihad to lift sanctions that the United Nations had imposed throughout the intervening years. Journalist Barbara Crossette reported that in the speech Saddam Hussein "seamlessly rewrote the history of January 17, 1991, by leaving out what had caused the war: his army's occupation of Kuwait five months earlier. . . . Iraq won that war, he said—still calling it 'the mother of all battles'— because 'Iraq refused to comply and surrender'" (Crossette 1998). Both sides declared and continue to declare victory.

What about those thousands of Iraqis who died? We have forgotten them because we have not heard the witnesses, those whose language "suggests the unimaginable of the real, that is, a hidden dimension that exceeds the strict limits of objective description" (Taminiaux 1993: 4–6). We must search for "the traces of the war so as to fight effectively its work of destruction" (17). Below are some traces of the unimaginable of the real that I have made out in the words of Iraqi and Kuwaiti women.

Gendering the Gulf War Story

In November 1995 I spent a week in Kuwait with Layla al-'Uthman, Kuwait's leading woman writer. We toured the war "sites": the rusty, bullet-riddled ship that had housed the Ramada Inn, the Kuwaiti National Museum, of which nothing remains but a burned-out shell. We drove past new buildings that had risen from the rubble. I heard about fires in the oil fields, and faces filmed over with black oil soot, months when it was always night, and electricity cuts, and then candles until they ran out of wax.

On the third evening Layla had a party. Everyone was singing and dancing. Around 3 A.M. the mood changed, became nostalgic, somber even. When I asked someone what was happening, he told me that the musicians had started to play Iraqi music. Everyone sat down and listened quietly. Soon they were gone. I had not noticed the change in the music. Next morning over coffee, Layla explained that the guests had become depressed because the music reminded them of the past and of what they had lost: "We were the same people: we shared music, food, and art as well as language—the southern Iraqi dialect is almost indistinguishable from the Kuwaiti."

But these neighbors had invaded. Journals I have received chronicle the war from the arrival of 100,000 Iraqi soldiers in Kuwait City on August 2, 1990, at 3 A.M. through January 17, 1991, the beginning of Desert Storm—a term the Kuwaitis also were using (al-Zibn 1993: 99)—until the Iraqi withdrawal on February 27. Communications were immediately cut, and the only contacts with the outside world were the international media, such as Reuters, BBC, and CNN. [Later, when the United States and its allies attacked, this would be true in Iraq also. The journalist Warid Badr al-Salim describes a night in Basra when the bombing was intense: "A night of constant broadcasts bringing news of the war blow by blow. The Allied planes kept on attacking various targets in Iraq and CNN." He then mentions Voice of America and Radio Monte Carlo, whose commercials for Mazola, fancy restaurants, and cars brought him a sense of well-being and even hope (1994: 48, 59).]

The Kuwaitis were in the war, yet like us halfway across the world, they knew it "only through the international media" (al-Zibn 1993: 117). The Iraqis quickly tightened their grip on the city, taking over the hospitals, surrounding the embassies, emptying the streets. Bread lines, hoarded food, public executions, arrests, house searches, expropriation of cars and apartments, water and power cuts, exploded oil wells, two million barrels of oil on the gulf. They even arrested members of the Red Crescent and stole their supplies. In November, "organized looting" began and civil registers were destroyed, as Kuwait became part of Iraq, and Kuwaitis had to submit a request for Iraqi identity cards. Men between the ages of seventeen and forty-five were arrested. Sports clubs were turned into prisons.

Despite the dangers, many Kuwaiti women stayed to endure the invasion while the men left. Moreover, they were the ones at the forefront of the resistance to the Iraqi invasion. Fatima Hussein, editor of the Kuwaiti daily newspaper *Al-Watan*, said that "the first anti-Iraq demonstration three days after the invasion was made up of only women and children. . . . Kuwaiti women played a major role in the Resistance." She compares their actions, which included smuggling arms and resistance documents, with those of Algerian women during their war of independence between 1954 and 1962: "they completely veiled themselves, which gave them a certain invisibility and enabled them to move quickly around the country more easily than men" (Goodwin 1995: 158–59). The Jordanian novelist Fadia Faqir writes of a woman whose vision of the receding skyline made her decide to stay in Kuwait. Regardless of the danger, she writes, "It is my country, where I belong, and where I should stay" (Faqir 1991: 81). What remains implicit in such a decision, but needs emphasis, is that there was a choice. Dalal Faysal Su'ud al-Zibn also realized that merely "staying in the country is a nationalist action for anyone who feels any sense of responsibility. . . . Whoever during times of trouble can think of something other than saving the nation does not deserve to live in a free state" (al-Zibn 1993: 128, 141). Here is the refrain from Arab women's writings on the wars they have experienced: When the country is in trouble, its citizens must stay.

The women who stayed in Kuwait throughout the fall of 1990 provided the needy with food, medical help, and logistical support in disposing of the dead and consoling the bereaved. They shared anger, grief, and the determination not to submit. In all that they did they risked imprisonment and even execution. Like the Lebanese, Palestinian, and Algerian women who stayed in their countries during their wars, these women constructed a "humanist nationalism" that interprets staying during a war as a form of combat—and combatants should be considered citizens with rights due to them (see cooke 1997: 267–90). Some Kuwaiti women accused those who left of having "forgotten their compatriots who stayed" (al-Zibn 1993: 162). Those who have forgotten those who stayed are not worthy of being considered Kuwaiti citizens.

As had happened during the Lebanese civil war, the violence drove some women to the pen for the first time. Three weeks into the air war, al-Zibn sees herself as a "writer." From the perspective of this new identity, she considers her experiences to be peculiarly important, useful for others: "I recorded these experiences so as to hold on to scattered thoughts and time . . . [and to] express what it is like to live the dailiness of war. There are few such [chronicles] and I believe that what I write will be important in the future!" At night she hides the journal lest the Iraqis steal it (63, 98, 135). Her journal has become valuable, worth stealing. In closing, she dedicates what she has come to call "memoirs" to "those who remained loyal to their country and their people" (171). This small, personal journal has been transformed into a big book of memoirs, as the author feels her relationship with her text and her readers develop. Writing them has made her experiences important and has transformed her into a witness.

Whereas some wrote for the first time, others, like Layla al-'Uthman, already an established writer, were silenced. It was not until 1994, three years after the war was over, that she published *Black Barricades*. These short stories evoke the shock of the invasion, its brutalities, the rape of mothers witnessed by their sons, the small acts of resistance and defiance. But within the mayhem, she bears witness to the odd innocence of the disoriented young Iraqis. The collection ends with nine sections, each entitled "Barricade." In each "Barricade," the narrator converses with Iraqi soldiers. One is almost apologetic about his presence, assuring her, "I curse the hour my feet stepped on this ground!" When she asks him why he came, he replies, "Orders!" When she is surprised that he asks for a cigarette and is not afraid that it might be poisoned, he replies, "We have already drunk poison over there."

"Where's there?"

"During the Eight Year War" (referring to the Iran-Iraq War).

"So you came to participate in a new war of liberation!!"

"You didn't need anyone to liberate you. You were free and we were envious."

"Do you know the truth?"

"I know it very well . . . I wish . . . Ah . . ."

"What do you wish?"

"That *Iraq* might be liberated" (al-'Uthman 1994: 149–51).

Other Kuwaiti women confirmed that the Iraqi soldiers were not simply inhuman enemies but rather victims. They were, of course, barbarian criminals sometimes, but they were also, as al-Zibn writes, "Saddam's misled animals [who] ran away from their war with Iran into the streets of Kuwait" (1993: 65–66). Like a pendulum, she swings between anger, maternal concern for the terrorized and alienated soldiers, and contempt for the leader who wanted Kuwait as a consolation prize for his failure against Iran. Saddam Hussein is one thing and the miserable creatures who have found themselves far from home and performing unspeakable acts are quite another.

These are the witnesses to whom we should listen: Kuwaiti women whose journals distinguish between the Iraqi people and their leader. Even as they were being victimized, they recognized that these soldiers were themselves victims. The Iraqi writer 'Amir Badr Hassun reports a conversation with a Kuwaiti intellectual who said to him, "Had we paid attention to what was happening to you and your people we might have protected our homeland from Saddam's occupation" (Hassun n.d.: 13).

The Iraqi Version

For the Iraqis, Gulf War II, as it was called, was part of a larger picture. Most would not know where to set the beginning of Gulf War I, because during the previous twenty years the military dictatorship in Iraq blurred, if not erased, the difference between declared and undeclared wars. Most Iraqis tell a story that describes several wars, which some divide into *two* Gulf Wars. Gulf War I begins with the 1968 takeover of power by the Revolutionary Command Council, whose leadership Saddam Hussein assumed in 1979.

Gulf War II was the war that made Dick Cheney proud. It lasted from January 16, when it still seemed possible that the war might not take place, to February 28, 1991, when the United States and its allies attacked al-Nasiriya and occupied the south of Iraq. It was presumed to mark the end of Gulf War I (Bhatia, Kawar, and Shahin 1992: 7). Warid Badr al-Salim's *Explosion of a Tear* (1994) follows a man as he moves restlessly around the country, picking up bits of news about the war. He is told that sons of neighbors and friends have left for Kuwait and that one of his brothers remains in the north with some troops—a sad reminder of the persistence of the Iran-Iraq War long beyond its presumed end (41–42). He witnesses an explosion and the havoc it wreaks, and he does nothing to help the victims. Then comes the black rain from the burning oil fields when, as Layla al-'Uthman described in Kuwait, day turns to night (79, 97–99). That is not the only reversal: after water and electricity in the psychiatric hospital are cut, the patients are released: "Imagine, you who have held on to your reason, how the war gave freedom to the crazy and stole it from the sane!" (81) Al-Salim ends with the army's withdrawal from Kuwait as they are targeted from above. The war victimizes equally Iraqis and Kuwaitis, men and women.

'Amir Badr Hassun's *The Book of Brutality* tells the story of the brutalization of an Iraqi woman intellectual from the middle of the Iran-Iraq War, and continues through the occupation of Kuwait and Gulf War II. Wars against neighboring countries change nothing in the habits of violence at home. Ms. Layla is tortured, and although she knows that if she, a law professor, can tell her story she "might contribute to the cause of the forgotten women prisoners in Iraq," she is not convinced that words can change anything, fearing rather that representation produces another form of violence, interesting the reader more than her suffering (Hassun n.d.; 12). "Can papers and words stop it?" she challenges Hassun, and he turns to us, his readers, and begs us to "shout even if into empty space because that is much better than silence. . . . People still react to calamities, they may even scream and demand that the cycle of terror and violence in Iraq be stopped" (70, 108–9).

Not all women were as skeptical of the power of the word as Ms. Layla. Despite heavy surveillance and a prohibition on criticism of any government venture in Iraq, some, like the poet Dunya Mikha'il, have written critically, if indirectly, of the regime. Mikha'il defied the minister of culture's 1989 warning against "writing in a surrealist style. . . . Surrealism is good for canvas but not in writing, where things should be clearly named. As for those who twist and move in a roundabout way, they are sick people and they must be kept under watchful eyes in order to analyse them to see how far this sickness goes" (Hazelton 1994: 18). In 1995 the Ministry of Culture's series of fiction on the Iran-Iraq War, called "Qadisiyat Saddam: Under Flames of Fire," published Dunya Mikha'il's forty-three-page *Journal of a Wave Outside the Sea*. Like others before her during the Iran-Iraq War, she succeeded in treading the fine line between writing for a government-sponsored literary series, evading the censor, and daring *not* to be patriotic (see cooke 1997, 220–66).

Mikha'il uses Greek mythology to veil her criticism of the leader and the state of war that has become the raison d'être of the Iraqi regime. She is telling an epic tale out of time and the region, which masks the immediacy of her political commentary. Some tiny creatures cower before the great god Zeus, who "amused himself by cutting stars out of heaven and pinning them on to shoulders. . . . His tigers pace up and down in their cages. At night they devour their prey and in the morning—when he walks in front of them—they mew" (Mikha'il 1995: 37). Zeus has a magic panoptical mirror that allows his image to be reflected at all times and in all places. This is the Zeus who sent Prometheus to steal fire from hell and who then burned him to death for having committed the theft. He it was who burned the clouds, scattered them on the waves, and when the waves became agitated enclosed them with barbed wire (38). Each Iraqi, Mikha'il suggests, has been turned into a wave outside the sea, into a "word wandering through dictionaries looking for a meaning for itself" (10). Each is tortured by the dread of death and by frightful memories.

Survival depends on the ability to forget, to unlearn language that unleashes war. Makha'il threw "the dictionary into the sea and watched the words grow with the circles and become encrusted with salt, changing MLH [*milh* means 'salt'] into HLM [*hulm* means 'dream']." Salt is interchangeable with dreaming. As a child, the poet had thrown a "stone into the sea and the letters and circles became agitated and they escaped out of my hands. At the height of their agitation, the letters BHR [*bahr* means 'sea'] spread out and then came together before me as HRB [*harb* means 'war']" (42). If the letters were already in the sea, then the dictionary must have been thrown before the stone, namely during her childhood. From the very beginning, from this precious period of freshness and innocence that is childhood, M-L-H and

B-H-R (the salt of the sea, the symbol of freedom) had always dissolved into H-L-M and H-R-B (dream and war). Dreaming was as dangerous to freedom as was war. The real "hell was never to awaken from the dream" (43), from war.

To escape the war-dream dilemma, she imagines herself to be God, creating first Good and then Evil, infusing life into the formless cell, separating the sun from the moon, and day from night: "I took a handful of earth and kneaded it with my tears and blew on it and it became a creature like me. I rested on the seventh day which I sanctified. But I became bored so I mixed fire, air, water and earth, and then I smelt the odor of war" (25). War, the outcome of boredom, was daily fare that none could escape, so that life was nothing other than a "bridge suspended between two wars" (14). Mikha'il echos Klaus Theweleit when she writes that wars don't end, they "reproduce themselves and destroy us" (24).

Mikha'il, Ms. Layla, al-'Uthman, al-Zibn. Here are some witnesses of the war Baudrillard said did not happen. These are the traces the U.S. government and media tried to disappear. When analyzing one of the most "problematic" events of the war, Andrew Whitley, head of Middle East Watch, explains that the Pentagon had been "queasy about the implications [of the February 25 massacre and so] the Western press and television, too, have made little of it" (Prochaska 1992: 91, 92). These Kuwaiti and Iraqi women remind the world of those it would forget: the Iraqi people who were held on January 17, 1991, the Night of Nightmares like a "bird strangled between two strongly shaking fists" (Mikha'il 1995: 12). The fist of Saddam and the fist of those who came "from the ends of the earth, like a circling eagle, a nation that does not understand your language . . . who will eat the fruit of your land until it is exhausted . . . will annihilate you" (32).

The Kuwaiti women's recognition that the men sent to brutalize them have themselves already been brutalized does not exonerate the men of their crimes but rather puts them into a context that helps understanding. The Iraqis were not fearsome members of the "fourth largest army in the world, an army hardened in long years of combat against Iran," to quote Cheney. They were victims of their government and leader. The Allied attack was merely another layer of cruelty laid on top of a habit of violence grown ordinary.

Migrating Stories

Beyond a preoccupation with war and violence, but sometimes also connected to it, Arab women have written about emigration. Since the mid-nineteenth century, Arabs from eighteen different countries have been migrating into Western Europe and the Americas. The first wave of immigrants into the United States was primarily Syrian, and it included in its numbers several women (Shakir 1997: 27–34). Most came with families, some were on their own. There must have been writers among the women, but we have only heard from men, like the Lebanese Gibran Khalil Gibran, and Mikha'il Nu'ayma, who created the Mahjar School in the United States, or the Egyptians Taha Hussein and Tawfiq al-Hakim, who studied in Paris.

As the rate of migration to Europe and the Americas increased because of economic and political necessity, diaspora literature grew, and recently it has come to include women like Ghada al-Samman, Hanan al-Shaykh, and Emily Nasrallah. Just as women were not supposed to be critical of their nations or men during war, so it seems they were not to write negatively about the diaspora experience. While men, like the Sudanese al-Tayib Salih, who spent several years in the West, could describe their alienation or their anger that might erupt into vengeful action, women generally wrote nostalgically about their places of birth.

During the 1990s this trend has changed as some Arab women have turned to their adopted countries for inspiration. The Syrian-born Ghada al-Samman, who moved from Lebanon to

Paris during the Lebanese civil war, first continued to write about Lebanon and its war. But then in 1994, almost ten years after establishing her residence in France, she published *The Square Moon*, a collection of stories that portray Arabs trying to adjust to their new life in Paris as though it were on a different, supernatural order from life in the Arab world.

In these stories that hover uneasily between reality and hallucination, the women generally fare better than the men, who risk dying surrounded by the accusing ghosts of those they have crushed on their way to the top (al-Samman 1998: 91). When the men fail, they may have to rely on the women they had previously forced to rely on them. The heroine of "The Swan Genie" struggles to reconcile her love for her spoiled husband with her happiness at having found meaning for her life in Paris. When the war forces the couple to leave Beirut, they find themselves penniless in Paris. His great wealth is tied up in Lebanese land made worthless by the war. To assure some income, she works and steadily rises to the top of the retail industry. He is humiliated by her successes, the family's dependence on her salary, and, above all, the awareness that their friends know of their plight and pity them. His one dream is that someday he will once again be able to afford their old life. When the war is over, his lands do indeed regain their value, and he imagines that things can go back to where they were. Returning to *status quo ante* means that he is back in charge of her life and that she is once again the bejewelled mannequin dispensing charity to the poor of Beirut. She, however, has experienced too much: "I no longer feel I am a stranger in Paris. . . . I feel like one who has betrayed an old lover named Beirut." It is not that she no longer loves Beirut but that she loves Paris too. She must now choose but feels she cannot: "When I am here, I feel I have betrayed Beirut; and when I go there, I feel Beirut has betrayed me!" (96) Emigration is not a simple matter of going somewhere else until you feel better and can return.

Emigration means that instead of being caught in one place, one is trapped in two places, each of which is home and is at the same time not home. Emigration means that wherever one is, one always longs to be in the other place. The only way to resolve this split between two places may be in writing. The words on the page may be the only way to bring these two places together in a way that does not cause pain and longing. This is what Hanan al-Shaykh does in her epistolary novel *Beirut Blues*. The heroine, Asmahan, writes letters—which she will probably not send—to friends, to lovers, to the land, to her grandmother, to the war, and to Beirut. They are letters from a woman who stayed in Beirut during the war and is now grappling with the experience. She is trying to understand how she and others have changed.

In the last letter Asmahan tells her girlfriend why she could not finally leave even when she had all that was necessary: the visa, the boyfriend, and the new life beckoning from Paris. She is in the airport VIP lounge with Jawad, the expatriate Lebanese writer who has won fame and fortune writing about the war far away from the war. She remembers how she used to feel about people like her who left. She "would be depressed for a few days and then get back" into her routine (al-Shaykh 1995: 328). When these people called her to ask what life was like, she knew they could not understand her. Those who left, blurring together for those who did not, soon found themselves ill at ease wherever they went. Jawad told Asmahan that the reason he returned to Lebanon was to see how much the country had changed and in its reflection how much he had changed: "Even if I tried, I couldn't live here any more and I feel the places themselves don't want me, but they're always in my mind and they stop me being content" (359). She decides at the last moment not to go, not "to turn into one of those pathetic creatures who are always homesick, always saying I wish I were still in Beirut. . . . I know I'm not happy here, but why should I be unhappy in two countries?" (366) Although it may feel to her as though this is the last moment she has to choose, or to think about the choice, it is not. Circumstances force both those who stay and those who leave to examine and rethink what they had thought were final choices.

Nothing compels attention to the choice more vividly than the return of the migrant. Since the 1960s and from the "Old Country," the Lebanese Emily Nasrallah has been observing the negative effects that the human drain of the Lebanese country-side has had on the community left behind. From her first novel, *September Birds* (1962), to *Sleeping Embers* (1994), Nasrallah has been examining the conflicting emotions of those who leave and those who are left. Excitement at the thought of a new life in the capital or abroad is usually counterbalanced for the migrant by anxiety and longing for what is irrevocably gone. Meanwhile, those who have stayed dream hopefully or jealously about life in the diaspora. How can Lebanese society flourish, Nasrallah seems to ask, if it is structured around the expectations that its sons, and sometimes its daughters, will leave to seek fame and fortune elsewhere?

Throughout the Lebanese civil war, Nasrallah insisted on the heightened need for the Lebanese to stay and not to continue their exodus with vague promises about returning. The war allowed her to reconfigure the nation as a village, a place of inti-mate belonging for all. Those who left their villages for Beirut were no longer abandoning home and roots, but rather were linking the capital to its provinces and rendering the boundaries between them porous (cooke 1988: 144–63). In 1981 Nasrallah wrote her first novel set outside Lebanon. *Flight Against Time* bridges the space between home and diaspora with an old peas-ant couple finally visiting their children in a Lebanese commu-nity in Prince Edward Island. The anticipated joy gives way to despair when they realize that their children have no intention of returning home. Their home is where they are in Canada. The father soon returns to Lebanon, dreading the cold death he would otherwise suffer in this cheerless place.

Thirteen years later Nasrallah published *Sleeping Embers* (1994). Was this the book she had long wanted to write? She had told me in 1982 that she was waiting for the moment when she might speak about the return of the September birds, those birds about which she had written in 1962. However, the lack of response from the diaspora, even at the height of the war, dulled the hope. The novel opens in the village of Jurat al-Sindyan, with Nuzha freshly returned with her Buick, big bucks, and bad Arabic. The second wife of Abdallah, a rich emigrant, she had married the fifty-year-old when she was sixteen. His age was immaterial as long as he helped her escape the village. Twenty-five years later, she returns to this timeless realm of cardamom coffee and thyme, sleeping in the shadow of Mount Hermon. Villagers come to her with anxious questions about their emigrant families, their heads filled with the same dreams of profit and escape that had motivated Nuzha. None more so than Dib, who invests his hopes in her, not caring, had not cared a quarter of a century earlier, about the age difference between them (Nasrallah 1994: 327). Nuzha stumbles around the village, trying to make up for the hurt she has involuntarily caused, but in the process causing more. At times, even the author seems to share the villagers' anxiety, describing Nuzha as calculating and vengeful when she loses the influence she once enjoyed.

Sleeping Embers is Nasrallah's first attempt to bring the emigrant home. The reader is able to enter the worlds of both and to see how far apart they have grown. Too much has happened after the emigrant's departure for there to be any real possibility of reconciliation, or even communication. Nuzha had hoped that bygones might become bygones and that somehow she might turn the clock back and start again. However, her every step is watched by the anxious villagers, who mistrust her open and free behavior, who cannot understand what it is that she wants but feel sure that she does not wish them well. Her intentions are consistently misconstrued. The good emigrant is the long-distance nationalist who stays away and sends home regular remittances (Anderson 1998: 58–74).

Nasrallah's earlier appeals to the emigrants to return and to assume their responsibilities to the needy country have been mitigated by her realization that the intention to leave one's birthplace and settle abroad carries indelible consequences. Those who return will be foreigners however much they want to be Lebanese. The time away will have made them forget how to behave, will have closed off the possibility of belonging once again to the community they had left. The gap between home and diaspora cannot be bridged. Each is its own world with its own rules and behaviors that grow increasingly distinct with time. For each the dream of the return cannot, indeed should not, come true. No matter how much individuals attempt to restore the fiction of an essential link between birth, land, language, and citizenship, the mapping of identity onto territory has become increasingly difficult in today's fragmented world.

Conclusion

The writers discussed above are tackling topics that were previously taboo, and international publishers have begun to sign them to their lists. For these women, there is a price to be paid, the price for which all globalizing projects must budget: How to balance the benefits of participating in late capitalism with the danger of being labeled westernized? In other words, how does the woman who once wrote viscerally out of the need to express her own and her community's urgencies now confront the writing project when she knows that even if she writes in the most obscure of Arabic vernaculars, she may see this once almost inaccessible text quickly translated into at least one UN language? How is she read? How is she marketed? The difference between

Hanan al-Shaykh's *The Story of Zahra* (1980) and *Women of Sand and Myrrh* (1988), with its appeal to exoticized notions of how Arab women behave in their special spaces of segregation, and which was translated almost immediately upon its release in Arabic, reflects al-Shaykh's awareness of her new global status.

These women are writing with the increased awareness that the information age has enabled a transnational literary project. To become an international writer means to become part of a community other than the one into which one was born, to write for it as much, if not more, than for one's birth community. This is not necessarily a bad thing. Some may find the international readership more neutral and less inhibiting, allowing them to write in a way not otherwise possible. Others may welcome the new readers who allow them to frame their issues more broadly. We might well ask whether the Algerian Assia Djebar, while she was writing her autobiographical novels *Fantasia: An Algerian Cavalcade* (1985), *A Sister to Sheherezade* (1986), and *Vaste est la Prison* (1995), was thinking only about the situation of Algerian women after the war of independence. Or did she recognize how her own condition of regret for having kept silent during war resembled that of her Iranian, Cambodian, or South African neighbors in her Paris apartment building? Does this globalization of Algerian women make their novels more effective? Or does the celebration of an Arab woman's writings in the West necessarily contaminate both the writer and the message so that the advantages gained from reaching a broader readership are outweighed by the risks of being accused of cultural betrayal and threatening national cohesion? There are a thousand and one ways to suppress women's writings. Somehow, and despite the neglect or negative criticisms of their work, Arab women continue to write.

2

In Search of Mother Tongues

utobiographies have become key sites for the questioning of norms and for the construction of alternative visions. As they examine the building blocks of their lives, writers, and especially women writers, are disentangling language, religion, place, and birth. They are asking what it means to call one particular language one's mother tongue when several languages are vying for primacy in establishing authentic identity. Arab writers in North Africa are examining the constructedness of language and of its supposedly natural links with identity and are showing how fragile are the connections said to undergird the unitary conception of identity.

Assia Djebar's Prisonhouse

In her semiautobiographical novel *Vaste est la Prison* (1995), Assia Djebar returns to her earlier preoccupation with Algerian women's actions during periods of nationalist resistance and their silence about this participation. We read about women whom Simone de Beauvoir and Frantz Fanon lionized in the 1960s, but whose voices were rarely, if ever, heard. Without their voices, these women remained abstract heroines who had sprung up, Venus-like, from the waves of the Algerian maquis. Djebar gives voice and reality to these women's struggles and frustrations and links them to their foremothers who must have also resisted the French when they arrived on the Algerian coast in the 1830s.

With surprising sympathy for European men who did not fully comprehend the consequences of their actions, she reads the documents they left behind and tries to understand their motivations and their mistakes. Ever since the seventeenth century, men had tried to identify and decode a mysterious script found on a tomb in Dougga in modern-day Tunisia. Their ineptness, due to their lack of access to the whole of society, fractured their knowledge and resulted in violence. They destroyed the site, and used the archaeological pretext to invade North Africa. Had they understood the role of women in Berber society, Djebar suggests, they might have been able to crack the unbreakable code without automatic resort to violence. In 1925 the puzzle was solved at the Sahara pilgrimage site of Abalessa. The ancient tomb of Tin Hinan, a Berber Tuareg princess, known for her military prowess, was discovered. Here was the same script, "as though the ancestral writing preserved outside the realm of submission was irreducible, moveable as its people who, supreme elegance, leave to their women the preservation of writing while their men make war" (148). This, writes Djebar, is the language of "the Berber queen who resisted the Arab conquest." The language of women is immediately connected with war and women's effective resistance to outside predators. Djebar describes this script as "our most secret writing, as ancient as Etruscan or the Runes, but unlike them it still resounds with the sounds and whispers of today. It is the legacy of women in the deepest space of the desert. Tin Hinan buried in the belly of Africa!" (164) This is a writing that precedes speech, and yet it contains today's sounds. It is in the contradiction of these women's language that its strength lies.

How could Djebar recognize this language? It had been passed down to her by her mother, but not as that specific language. Its legacy survived in "some details in the embroidery of women's costumes, as a light accent deforming the local dialect and preserved for as long as possible as the sole residue, an Arab-Andalusian vernacular." This women's language lived on as lute music, and also as a "vacillating luminosity crossing the centuries and perpetuating the light of the Andalusia of women" (170). This language of embroidery, of accent, of music and of light created the poetry of the Andalusian Noubas that her mother had memorized without being able to read the books in which it was recorded. Although she could not write, this knowledge made her literate.

Djebar's vivid and poetic evocation of a writing that precedes sound and orality recalls the "arche-writing" that Jaques Derrida theorized as being "at work not only in the form and substance of graphic expression but also in those of non-graphic expression. It would constitute not only the pattern uniting form to all substance, graphic or otherwise, but the movement of the sign-function linking a content to an expression, whether it be graphic or not." This arche-writing becomes embodied in the *trace* that

> does not depend on any sensible plenitude, audible or visible, phonic or graphic. It is, on the contrary, the condition of such a plenitude. . . . *The trace is in fact the absolute origin of sense in general. Which amounts to saying once again that there is no absolute origin of sense in general.* . . . And as it is *a fortiori* anterior to the distinction between regions of sensibility, anterior to sound as much as to light, is there a sense in establishing a 'natural' hierarchy between the sound-imprint, for example, and the visual (graphic) imprint? (Derrida 1976: 60, 62, 65; original emphasis)

This condition of plenitude that anticipates the distinction of language into graphs and sounds but that is necessarily a writing characterizes the poetry and accompanying musical annotation that Djebar had read in some of her mother's books. These books were not read but only exhibited as a special legacy. Because they were not used, they functioned more as icons, new appearances of the trace.

During the Algerian war of independence, Assia's mother left Algeria to visit her son in a prison in France. During this absence, some French soldiers burst into her apartment and tore the books. Djebar implicitly compares this vandalism to that of the archaeologists because, like their predecessors, these twentieth-century French soldiers could not decipher this writing of women and, interpreting it to be "the message of some nationalist connivance" (Djebar 1995: 171), destroyed it. The secrets of this women's language frighten these men, and fear makes them dangerous. With all their knowledge and power, the men from the north do not know how to decipher North African women's secrets. They do not have access to the heart of what for them must remain darkness. And this ignorance makes them crazy, violent.

The lost language of Tin Hinan passed down as light, embroidery, and music became Algerian women's mother tongue. Djebar writes that this "archaic alphabet" (164) is "inscribed in a tongue that is certainly maternal" (158). The tearing of the books once again threatened the "maternal heritage" with extinction because although Djebar's mother knew the words and the music, her daughter did not. Because she was illiterate, Djebar's mother could not teach her how to write poetry, and so she had to find a way to recover and encode it. This way winds between the oral and the written. This mother tongue is associated with sound, "the secret vibration so as to reach me had to pass through the sister's love" (304). But it is a sound that functions as a "sound-image," which is not the actual, physical sound, but what Derrida calls "the psychic imprint of the sound" (1976; 63). This sound-image becomes language when it is apprehended by a sister, a woman like Djebar who writes in a language that is felt before it is thought. The language of these sisters when written is the mother tongue: "Did I say 'mother tongue,' when I should instead have evoked this sororal echo or its capsizing"? (Djebar 1995: 304). Djebar writes this mother tongue so as to resist the urge of history to silence women and the language they spoke and still speak: "After long writing on the dead of my land in flames, last century, I believed that the blood of men today (the blood of history and the stifling of women) was rising up again to stain my writing and to condemn me to silence." This is not rhetoric. Djebar presents herself as the link between the Berber princess who resisted the Arab conquest and the women in Algeria's civil war today.

Algerian women have been at the forefront of the fighting in this religious war. Women intellectuals, journalists, university professors, and doctors have both resisted and supported the Islamists. Malika Mokeddem's *L'Interdite* (1993) tells of Algerian women's struggles against the Islamists in the 1990s. The novel ends with women in a desert settlement ganging up against the men on behalf of Sultana, the free-spirited native daughter recently returned from Montpellier. Sultana claims no credit but rather observes that she had merely expedited a process already in place.

Djebar is less optimistic than Mokeddem about the possibilities for women's activism, but she does invest hope in their writing. The risks notwithstanding, Djebar knows that she too must write/speak so that her own as well as these women's writings/voices will not be lost (Djebar 1995: 337–45). She marks the success of their resistance when she writes, "Finally, all of us, women from the shadows, we are reversing the direction of movement, watching, we are making a new beginning. . . . The women, the ones who were forgotten because they were without writing, are forming the funeral march, the new Bacchantes" (175, 338). So as not to be one of the forgotten, Djebar knows that she must learn how to speak and at the same time to write even if it be with blood: "The blood of my writing? Not yet, but my voice? My voice leaves me every night" as she awakens the voices of kinswomen she had known as a child but can only now understand (337).

As in her *Fantasia*, she finds herself trying to scream, not quite succeeding, and being alarmed by the sound she has produced. Her cry contains the suffering of others and then lifts her like a bird in vibrant, blind flight. As she feels her ancestors push her forward, the words of "the lost language" rise up out of them to create an oppositional legacy. Meanwhile the men gesticulate in the killing fields (339). This is her weapon, this French perfumed with the stitches and light of the mother tongue. It recognizes and revives *les cris* and *l'écrit* of the women killed throughout history for having dared to express themselves. Her French mixed with the poetry of the Andalusian Nubias and the whispers of the writing of Tin Hinan becomes the mother tongue.

Writing becomes lost tongue becomes whispers becomes writing. These traces of resistance and vestige chiseled into the rock of a stele abandoned in the desert become silence for the men, but whispers for the women. Here are the *atlal*, or effaced traces of the beloved's encampment in the desert, a trope of pre-Islamic poetry. Lost traces of women transformed this writing into an oppositional heritage. These traces retained the living echo of the whispers of the writing that came from and in turn created the mother tongue. Djebar's fluid, dynamic language occupies the space between loss and a new beginning. This language forms the basis of a kind of nation, a nation of women. This language-as-nation provides a space of safety and belonging.

There is nothing of the natural in this mother tongue, nothing of blood and birth. This is a tool of power that allows women to link themselves in a chain of women through time and space. And because it is not mysteriously part of one's identity, but rather a conscious creation, it is not hemmed in with doubts and anxieties. If the mother tongue does not mark the site of authentic identity then the adoption of another language will not form the existential threat that it did for some, like the Tunisian Jew Albert Memmi (b. 1921) and the Palestinian Christian Anton Shammas (b. 1949), as well as postcolonial writers such as the Moroccan Muslim Abdelkebir Khatibi (b. 1937) and the French Jew Jacques Derrida. These men have written semiautobiographical books that examine aspects of their intellectual trajectories refracted through the prism of language. In the case of each of these male writers, I have marked religious identity because of its role in disentangling the apparently natural relationships among language, birth, culture, and citizenship. These men fight nostalgia for the mother tongue so as to be able to negotiate their existential, but also political, relationship with the hegemonic language.

Albert Memmi's Struggles with His Mother

Three years before Tunisian independence, Albert Memmi published in French his *Pillar of Salt* (1953), which examines the experience of Tunisian Jews under French rule. Thirty-two years later in the eastern Mediterranean, Anton Shammas published *Arabesques* (1985) in Hebrew, the language of the Israeli state in which he lived as a barely tolerated minority. Each book, written in the hegemonic language, foregrounds the role of this language in the shaping of identity and citizenship. Memmi writes of French as having a "magic spell of language" (1955: 32), and Shammas refers to Hebrew as the "language of Grace" (1985: 92). The illusion in each case is that mastery of the imposed language will create a new identity that accrues special civic privileges otherwise unobtainable. Language holds out the hope that birth and religion can be overcome. In a 1988 lecture, Shammas said, "Territories of the Hebrew language, formerly strictly Jewish, are now being counter-occupied, as it were, by non-Jewish Hebrew speakers, thereby making Hebrew less Jewish and more Israeli." *Arabesques* had not yet been classified as an Arab novel in Hebrew, and Shammas could at that time still hope that this literary tour de force would make him an Israeli in a way he could not otherwise be. The Hebrew was admired and the book well received, but not as an Israeli novel. The book experiment ultimately proved to Shammas that non-Jews could never become fully Israeli, however well they assimilated to the dominant norms. In an early 1990s interview with Smadar Lavie he is categorical in assessing the result of the experiment: "For the non-Jewish Arab writer, Ashkenazi Hebrew is not only the homeland of the Jews—it's the language of threat. . . . I tried . . . to bring about a new version of Israeli identity, but I couldn't make it happen outside the text. I wrote in the language of the territory. I approached the territory and told her, Territory, come on—is your language Hebrew? Great!

I'll write in it. Are you going to give me part of yourself?" (Lavie 1996: 85) She did not.

Whereas for Shammas the process of social and civic exclusion passed through the writing of the book, its publication and reception, for Memmi it is enacted in the text itself. The protagonist of *Pillar of Salt*, Alexandre Mordechai Benillouche, is aware, even as a child, that language is not neutral but rather is an instrument of power. To be restricted to Arabic, especially the spoken version, which in North Africa particularly is far from the high language of the Qur'an, meant social and economic stagnation. To master French promised escape from such a condition. When he goes to high school, Benillouche models himself on his French teacher, M. Marrou, "himself a Berber by birth and family background, though a Christian as a consequence of his upbringing." Despite the fact that Marrou is resented by his French colleagues, he symbolizes for the young Benillouche the ability to overcome one's origins. His disconcertingly beautiful poems demonstrate "that it is possible to achieve a true mastery of a language that is not one's mother tongue. . . . Marrou helped me to understand what kind of an individual I am" (Memmi 1992: 219, 224). So when Marrou asks the class for Racine's most typical line in *Andromaque* and Benillouche answers correctly, he is thrilled that "I, son of an Italian-Jewish father and a Berber mother, had discovered in Racine's work the line that is most typical of Racine" (113).

But these successes are necessarily temporary and partial. Failure to master the hegemonic language and to cull its promised fruits of full citizenship was built in to the structure of the colonizing system. Expressions and performances of self-loathing could not provide entry into the master group. One might at best live in the borderlands between both cultures. This was the condition of Jews in North Africa to whom the French gave citizenship throughout the nineteenth century.

Flirting with the possibility of multiple belongings, Tunisian Jews in fact experienced plural exclusions. Every language that Benillouche spoke alienated him from the community that laid claim to that language:

> My mother tongue is the Tunisian dialect, which I speak with the proper accent of the young Muslim kids of our part of town and of the drivers of horse-trucks who were customers of our shop. The Jews of Tunis are to the Moslems what the Viennese are to other Germans: they drag out their syllables in a singsong voice and soften and make insipid the guttural speech of their Mohammedan fellow-citizens. The relatively correct intonations of my speech earned me the mockery of all: the Jews disliked my strange speech and suspected me of affectation, while the Moslems thought I was mimicking them. But when I entered school, it was no longer a matter of shades of pronunciation but of a total break. (Memmi 1992: 30)

Memmi anticipates Derrida's paranoia about pronunciation, the fine shades of accent that betray the one who wants to "pass" but who is doomed to remain attached to that which he has been taught to despise. The only way out was not to speak until he had crushed the mother tongue and perfected the written French. Alarming experiences with spoken French taught him that he might always remain "a native in a colonial country, a Jew in an anti-semitic universe, an African in a world dominated by Europe. . . . I discovered I was doomed forever to be an outsider in my own native city. And *one's home town can no more be replaced than one's mother*" (96; my emphasis). The mother is both the closest but also the most distant person. Benillouche racializes and intellectualizes the difference between himself and his mother. Because she is Berber she can physically tolerate the sun better than he can; because she is illiterate he convinces himself that he cannot communicate with her. Yet she remains his conscience, censoring his empty arrogance. However uneducated she might be, she constantly reminds him that he cannot escape who he essentially is.

The greater the hold of the mother, the more urgent becomes the need to overcome her and the language with which she is associated. If he ceases to think in the mother tongue then it may cease to interfere with his mastery of French. The turning point comes when Beuillouche brings Poinsot, his philosophy teacher, home. He is trying to connect the two poles of his life: philosophy and his mother. But this meeting between his teacher and his mother merely reinforces the separation and drives him "to choose one of them. Between the East and the West, between African superstitions and philosophy, between our dialect and the French language, I now had to choose" (229). He chooses philosophy. The choice helps to unblock the French language. Toward the end of the book he congratulates himself on forgetting his Arabic and thinking only in French: "I now belong to Western culture and would be incapable of writing or expressing myself satisfactorily in Arabic" (265). The echos from Fanon ring loud and clear: "To speak means to be in a position to use a certain syntax, to grasp the morphology of this or that language, but it means above all to assume a culture, to support the weight of a civilization. . . . To speak a language is to take on a world, a culture" (Fanon 1967: 17–18, 38). Benillouche speaks French and has taken on its world, its culture. He has shaped a single, monolingual identity. Finally he feels safe and strong.

Abdelkebir Khatibi's Bi-langue

Memmi is not alone to rejoice in the loss of the mother tongue: halfway through his philosophical autobiography, *Amour Bilingue*, the Moroccan Abdelkebir Khatibi also celebrates the fact that his mother tongue "lost" him (Khatibi 1990: 66). Unlike Memmi, who crushes his mother tongue, Khatibi is trying to escape its hold. Both are driven by the need to separate themselves from Arabic and to master French.

They emphasize writing, for there is much to be feared from speaking, the domain of the mother tongue. Unlike Djebar, who cherishes the whispers and music of the spoken, Memmi and Khatibi dread it. Speech is to be overcome so as to enable writing. Speaking is a dangerzone because of the lack of control over one's tongue. Like Djebar's mother tongue that is both silent (writing-trace) and filled with sound, Khatibi's is absent even as it is doubly present. He is not as fearful as Memmi, who hoped that his own language would not continue to speak, even if in silence, yet he too distrusts linguistic simultaneity. Khatibi considers this to be a particular problem for the Arab who writes in French because of the forced nature of the bilingualism. He has to fight against the loss of all the languages he knows: "he does not possess his mother tongue which cannot be written, nor the written language which is alienated and given to a substitution, nor this other language which has been learned and which threatens to deterritorialize itself in itself and to erase itself" (Khatibi 1985: 189). To speak one language does not eliminate the other but threatens it with irremediable transformation.

Like Memmi, Khatibi connects the mother tongue with his mother and his need to escape her: "I don't know what unavowed and hidden conflict existed between my mother and my birth. In time, doubles for my mother became indispensable to me so that I could confirm my genealogy-less screenplay. Not, as is said, so that I could return to the belly of the Mother my dead father and my invisible god had impregnated at the same time; but in order to accompany my real mother to the end of her days and her death" (Khatibi 1990: 91; see Khatibi 1985: 183). Khatibi buries his mother, hoping thus to sever the umbilical cord still binding him to his mother tongue. It is then that he can imagine a new birth that might dispense with the need for the body of the mother. Then he might be one of those who live in the "abyss of language . . . so pure as to be almost untranslatable" (Khatibi 1990: 21). Failure to escape the mother tongue is written into this space also. The untranslatable, Khatibi writes elsewhere, is not the

> "unspeakable, inaudible beyond that is doomed to remain closed forever. It is rather a labor of sleep and insomnia, hallucinating all translations and dreaming from language to language. . . . The mother tongue cannot disappear from the syntax of the body. . . . Driven back, silenced in the chasm of memory, this speaking flows back to scatter throughout the texture of the book. It forgets itself without forgetting itself, playing with the author: a history of amnesia . . . history of a palimpsest, of something that works beneath the white page, the erasure that springs forth out of the trace. . . . Such a text is double because it is supported silently and on a lost foundation by the mother tongue" (Khatibi 1985: 186, 188, 194–95).

Here is Djebar's mother-tongue-as-trace. In Amour Bilingue the untranslatable forces the mother back into a state of semiconsciousness that Khatibi calls the bi-langue. It is the mystical space of the unthought in every language (1990: 5), it is "the incommunicable" (35) before it has been codified into the communicable, where the substitution of one word for another was not a mistake but rather "speaking two words simultaneously: one which reached her hearing . . . and a second word, an other, which was there and yet was faraway, a vagabond, turned in upon itself. . . . I found that I was a stranger in my native language and that you were a stranger in yours" (28, 82). What Khatibi is suggesting is a kind of performative contradiction, for if the bi-langue is the space of the untranslatable where two languages come together, become strange to themselves, how can it be thought or spoken or defined?

Khatibi is taking his reader on a mystical journey experienced through various degrees of linguistic immersion in the *bi-langue*.

It is a sea in which he swims throughout the autobiography. When he almost drowns, he returns enlivened. This annihilation is the Sufi state of *fana'* that Khatibi describes as a "motherly word" (46). He even uses the technical term *fana'*, which he defines as presence at "death and to inhabit it on his behalf, and yet, faced with death, to carry away his living force. He destined himself for a test of the inexpressible, there where the word 'mort' embraces the word 'fana' (extinction), where both will find a place in the epigraph to his story, with no other tie than the gesture of an erasure" (46).

Developing the mystical analogy, Khatibi presents a place that is noplace where language is plural before it splits into languages: "He wanted to link himself to the language before beginning to braid the thinking for the *bi-langue* . . . different from all thought which affirms itself and obliterates itself in translation . . . my *bi-langue* of obliteration" (36, 67–68). In that space languages are not demarcated from each other, but continue simultaneously in each other's borderzones, always translating without translating, always themselves and other.

In the mystical sea of the *bi-langue*, the mother tongue does not threaten, for it is part of a linguistic whole. Wandering in and across the borders, Khatibi the postmodern nomad frees himself to "go off and stay: I am therefore detached. . . . The Orient—ah yes!—is my home, therefore I disorient myself toward other continents" (Khatibi 1990: 116). He has located himself in, but also away from, the global and the local simultaneously and without contradiction or ambivalence.

Jacques Derrida: "Le Petit Juif Français d'Algérie"

Jacques Derrida challenges the assertion that individual languages can be transcended by recourse to the source of language. There is first a major existential problem to be solved: "One must already know in which language the 'I' is said, I say myself . . . the

I-myself of the 'I remind myself' produces and offers itself differently according to the language spoken. It never precedes them, it
is thus never independent of language in general" (Derrida 1996:
54). There is then language to invent as the "I" is being imagined
and articulated. How can you narrate your life story when you are
not sure of your relationship to the language in which you are
forced to articulate your "I"? In contrast with Khatibi, who savors
the oscillation between languages and identities, Derrida finds no
joy in the hyphen of the "franco-maghrebin" that does not link his
two birth identities but rather estranges them. The hyphen highlights the memory of "protests, the cries of anger or of suffering,
the clash of weapons, planes and bombs" that connect the French
and the North Africans in a history of violence (30, 27). In an odd
contest over who is the "most essentially franco-maghrebin" of the
two of them, Derrida makes the surprising claim that he is more so
than Khatibi. Indeed, he is "perhaps the only franco-maghrebin"
(27–29). He has authorized himself to decode what such an identity
might mean. It means to have no language. Not one. Certainly not
two. Derrida, the great scholar of the French language and of language in general, declares that he has no language he can call his,
only one that belongs to another and on which he must draw.

Derrida insists on an absolute but always uncertain monolin-
gualism: "Je n'ai qu'une langue, [or] ce n'est pas la mienne." I
have one language only, and it is not mine. This is the theme of
his semiautobiographical reflection *Le Monolinguisme de l'Autre*
(1996): two negative possessives. It is not that language is not
owned, but that one can never oneself be the owner. Language,
always and necessarily in the singular, belongs to another—even
the colonial master, however hard he tries, can only convince
himself that he possesses a language through "an unnatural
process of politico-fantastic constructions." He can at best *pre-
tend* that the language is his (45).

Derrida refuses Khatibi's carnivalesque description of multiple
linguistic adoptions that do not evoke loss but pleasure and

power. Derrida finds Khatibi's assertion "that his mother tongue has lost him" (63) to be reason not for joy but for "grief." He uses the English word "grief," claiming that it is untranslatable. No other language can conjure up "the kind of mourning for something that one never had because I have never been able to call French, this language that I speak, 'my mother tongue'!" (60 –61) He had thought that he was French, but he did not possess French because he was not quite French. He was a "français d'Algérie" (77), "un petit Juif français d'Algérie" (82–83), a "pied noir" (80), and even only a "juif indigène" (72), a generic Jew from a place to which he was indigenous. Each added or subtracted qualifier had linguistic implications, so that one was more or less welcomed into or excluded from a linguistic community according to ascribed identity.

In his case the exclusion was not explicit, not legally enforced (58–59, 66). The story begins in 1870, when the French promulgated the Crémieux Decree that gave Algerian Jews French citizenship. They were thus distinguished from other Algerians, who had been considered French nationals, although not citizens, since the 1834 ordinance that annexed "French possessions in North Africa" (Derrida 1997: 127). From one day to the next, Jews—French or Arab or Berber—who had before been assimilated into their Arab or Berber communities stopped speaking Arabic or Berber. It was not that there was a law against learning Arabic, Berber, or even Hebrew; it was that these newly French Jews living on the borders of the Arab quarters—as did Derrida's grandparents (Derrida 1996: 66)—were steered away from those languages that they had spoken as *indigènes*. As newly French they were taught to despise these mother tongues. Without formal prohibition on the language there was little incentive to rebel, no need to imagine an alternative nation. They were merely thrown into what Derrida calls "trouble de l'identité" because they had become French, but then again not quite French, because to be truly metropolitan French was to be

Catholic (59, 87). Then in 1941 under Vichy, the indigenous Jews lost their citizenship for two years. In 1943 they regained it after Pétain was ousted (34–35). For two years Derrida had been deprived of a home, a mother country, and he had not even felt it. But then that was not new.

In all of his ascribed identities, Derrida was denied a home because he was denied a mother tongue. Because although he might be French, provisionally and conditionally so, he was also a native of Algeria and above all he was a Jew. As Memmi, another Jewish franco-maghrebin, and Shammas have written, religion matters in language. Derrida claims that the French people made those who were born in the colonies feel that the only language that they should speak was French, but that as franco-maghrebins they were destined never to speak it quite right, not in a pure accentless way that might establish a relationship of belonging.

Derrida undermines Memmi's contention that the French colonizers were all basically the same, all Christian. They were at one end of the spectrum, the Muslim Arabs or Berbers were at the other end, and everyone else took their place between them. Rank was established according to degree of acculturation and successful mimicry. Derrida, on the other hand, breaks down the assumed homogeneity of the colonizers by marking religion. The chasm between the French and the Jews, those almost-but-doomed-never-to-be-quite French, is as unbridgeable as it was for the colonized, but more painful. The Arabs, the Berbers, and other Mediterranean populations had their own nations, "seemed to have" their own languages, mother tongues to which they might have recourse when they recognized that the failure to mimic successfully was built into the system. What of the French Jew born in Algeria? Denied Algerianness because he was French, he was denied Frenchness because he was a Jew. What nation could he call his? What mother tongue offered itself? In an almost wistful way he remarks that there was no Hebrew (100), Yiddish, or Ladino for the Algerian French Jew (90–91).

The predicament of the French Jew born into a North African colony suggests that language may be disentangled from citizenship, from nationality, from culture, and from birth, even as it is said to be inextricably tied to them (31). How do you deal with the fact that the language you speak as the only language possible, as a mother tongue, is a language others claim as their specific, exclusive property? The answer for Derrida, as it was for Memmi, Shammas, Khatibi, and even for Djebar, seems to be in writing. For the in-between, nationless, stateless that was Derrida and are today the many millions of migrants who wander the globe, *writing* may be the only language they can own. This written language is their only nation: "a kind of loving, desperate appropriation of the language and thereby of a prohibiting-prohibited 'parole' (which French was for me) and beyond to all forbidden idiom. The loving, jealous vengeance" (59). The only thing worse than being an in-between, nationless, and stateless person is to be an *illiterate*, in-between, nationless, and stateless person. Derrida is calling for what Djebar has struggled with: the possiblity of translating *les cris* into *l'écrit*. Like her, he talks of the ugliness of his voice that had for so long been silent: "I was the first to be afraid of my voice as though it were not mine, to contest it, to hate it" (81).

Derrida's project is to show how language is free of notions of ownership. French is no more the property of the French people than it is of the Senegalese, of the Moroccans, of Khatibi, of Derrida himself (70, 127). When he writes of his own "grief" at the loss of something he never owned, he slips from his individual situation to that of others, bidding all to attend to their own griefs: "Listen . . . do not believe so easily, believe me, that you are a people" (61). Individuals must constantly renegotiate their relationship with the group. Nothing, not even—or, perhaps, particularly—language, can be taken for granted as providing an essential bond with others. It is a matter of reevaluating who one is vis-à-vis those with whom one lives. Is one the host or the guest or a stranger?

Identity and human relationships are structured in terms of hospitality. In such a scheme no one belongs naturally anywhere but is always working out the rights and responsibilities of "invitation, welcome, asylum, shelter" (Derrida 1997: 119). What are the rules specific to particular cultures that allow the host to question the guest and vice versa? When does the guest violate the rules and displace the host-become-hostage in a series of "substitutions that make of each and every one a hostage of the other. These are the laws of hospitality" (111)? When does the host flaunt these same rules and deny the guest rights due to guests? Which language mediates between these various persons and conditions?

These are not idle questions but vital precepts that form the basis of conviviality. We must understand and then learn these rules so that we might become citizens in the lands and languages that we inhabit as guests. Far from connoting ownership or belonging, language is "the experience of *expropriation*. The language said to be the 'mother tongue' is already the 'language of the other'" (83). One can at best fantasize ownership. For just as language seems to be that which remains the closest to the self and "does not leave me, it is also, *in reality and of necessity*, beyond fantasm, that which never ceases leaving me" (85). Language is centrifugal, always moving toward another whose language has determined the language we use. Our language must be that of our interlocutor if we wish to communicate. We are, therefore, always at the mercy of others, particularly when they have power, who may decide that, because of some characteristic, such as race or religion, we do not belong and that therefore we cannot own anything in that territory. Not land. Not language. Lack of linguistic ownership is demonstrated through imperfect performance. Rules of correctness are invented and increasingly applied as processes of exclusion intensify. What matters then is not who owns the language but who masters the rules of hospitality so as to preempt usurpation of citizenship, religion, language, and ultimately identity.

Conclusion

For each of these writers, the mother tongue is at the core of identity but also separate from it. The language that is believed to define the deepest level of who one is may in fact be a language imposed or assumed. How can we account for the different attitudes of these writers to their mother tongues? I would propose gender, historical context, and religion. First, men and women have radically different attitudes toward the mother tongue, which they may love, fear, or manipulate. Second, the negotiability of the mother tongue is obscured under colonialism because of the weight of the foreign culture and its absolute rules about who can and should speak which languages. Third, religion as an identity marker may determine whose language confers power on whom.

For colonized men, distance from the colonizer's language entails distance from power. The mother tongue is disdained because it is oral, the language of the illiterate. There is lexical support for this attitude: in Arabic, the mother tongue is *lugha ummiya*, whose meaning is both "maternal" and "illiterate" language. Yet *lugha ummiya* is not the Arabic term for mother tongue. The most common translation for mother tongue is *lughat al-umm*, or the "tongue/language of the mother." This possessive construction overcomes the uncomfortable overlap in the adjectival phrase that I have used, which confuses, or, better, highlights the connection between mother tongue and illiteracy. To use the mother tongue implies illiteracy and restriction to the realm of the spoken. Implicit also is the suggestion that the speaker of the mother tongue remains attached to the mother, dependent, a child under the paradoxical influence of the wild, primitive woman who is weak in every respect except in her terrifying role as mother of sons. Therefore the mother tongue has to be crushed so that it cannot interfere with the acquisition of the colonizer's language. Identity must be shaped by one language only, that of the powerful.

During the independence period, the struggle for true decolonization continued and with it came a change in the process of negotiation between multiple languages. Arabic and French are no longer considered to be absolute vehicles of expression but can be constructed in terms of each other so that they may become strange to those who had assumed their ownership. Memmi's case is particularly interesting because of the ways in which he has wavered over time in his attitude toward the mother tongue. In 1996, forty years after Tunisian independence, Memmi thinks back to his experience with language and he finally gives the mother tongue space: "I am less convinced that we must only be attached to a single language. The question of the mother tongue is obviously very emotional, very much linked to childhood memories. . . . I do think people must have the right to speak their native language. But I no longer think that all languages must be functional languages" (Wilder 1996: 174). In the September 1996 issue of *Le Monde Diplomatique*, he writes of the need for a deep communal identity to unite people into a modern nation. Such an identity is imagined and then tied up "with collective myths: myths of origin, myth of a homogeneous past, myth of a mother tongue, myth of common ancestors, myth of a future that is necessarily common, homogeneous and indivisible" (12). Two years later, he once again corrects himself, writing that the mother tongue is not so much a myth but rather a "reservoir of emotions and shared dreams and thus the most propitious for communion. . . . What is to become of mother tongues or national languages? They will survive as long as they serve a function: the mother tongue is the language of emotion and of the most intimate expression; the national language is the language of culture and administration. But the universal language will be the code necessary for communication, for the sciences and technologies. . . . Let us, therefore, rejoice in our mother tongues, let us defend our national languages, and let us teach our children the language spoken by the largest numbers of people" (1998: 2). Memmi has gone beyond his youthful terror of bilingualism to advocate multilingualism with an unprecedented celebration of the mother tongue.

Djebar's attitude to the mother tongue is quite different. She insists on the primordiality of her mother tongue passed down to her through generations of women going back to a Tuareg Berber warrior princess. Djebar is strategically positing a women's language that can be drawn on as a resource. This language that she learned from her mother is first of all a writing-trace that may be intuited in sounds, in embroidery designs, in light, and it is always already a new writing. To speak this language is to assume its culture, to support the weight of its civilization. Watching fellow Algerian women intellectuals being killed because of their writing, because of their mother tongue, she must find a way to combat their disappearance. She has discovered a language that belongs to her and to other resisting women. It is so much theirs that they need not know its grammar, syntax, or even vocabulary. They need only remain open to its rhythms. Even if she writes in French, she is not writing in the language of the other because she is recreating in this French a life lived by her foremothers in Berber and Arabic. She has "translated" French into her mother tongue, a writing-trace that becomes the basis of a new imagined community of women.

If the mother tongue is a resource of solidarity and power for potential mothers, it is a threat for the sons. Derrida's terrible discovery is that his French is not his, nor was it ever. Utterly alienated from his culture and his language, he suggests that the mother tongue should be recognized for what it is: a myth dreamed up by the powerful as a pretext for excluding whomever they wish. As a *langue matrice*, the abstract notion of a place of generation that would not be attached to the body of the mother, the mother tongue can become an instrument of identity, subjectivity, and power.

In contrast with male writers, Djebar has transcended the trauma of language as possession or tool of exclusion. She has revealed its generative and creative power. As we shall see in the next chapter, this is the language that she uses when she writes her story of the Algerian past and of the beginning of Islam and of women's uninterrupted activism. This is the language that fills the gaps that historians have created.

3

Reviewing Beginnings

Arab writers are disentangling language, blood, ethnicity, religion, and gender, and they are demonstrating that the apparently natural connections between them are in fact constructed and contingent. There is no fixed, essential center that would mark the core of a single, foundational identity. Throughout the twentieth century there has been much talk of identity: losing identity to imposed cultures and their values; uncovering lost identity; regaining authentic identity; asserting identity as member of a disadvantaged group; identity politics. In each case, identity is tied to birth, to place, to language, to community, to religion, and to gender. Identity confers rights. Identity takes rights away. But what is this singular, unified identity? If identity is the recognition of sameness with some and difference from others, then we have many identities. To retain a sense of wholeness, we usually assert only one of many possible identities, the one that gives authority at the moment of its assertion. This speaking position is not an identity, but rather an ascribed or chosen identification.

Most recently, religious identification has taken on political significance in postcolonial Arab countries. Social, economic, military, and political failures have galvanized reactionary, religious responses to Western domination, globalization, and the corrupt values they are thought to be spreading. Islamist groups from Morocco to Bahrain are calling for an Islamic state, within which they will reestablish what they consider to be Islamically sanctioned gender relations. What they are calling for is a jihad, understood as the individual-collective struggle within the Muslim society, which, even if it does not connote military war, does suggest the conditions pertaining to war. In other words, to be in a state of jihad is to be in a war-like state of emergency that demands a suspension of norms and the improvisation of new rules of conduct. As in times of war, these emergency conditions open up the possibility for changing expectations connected with women's roles and rights.

As we shall see in the next chapter, Zaynab al-Ghazali declared her right to participate in jihad. The Saudi preacher Fatima Naseef goes further to claim this right on behalf of all Muslim women. She dedicates a section in her chapter on women's political rights to the "Right to Participate in Jihad." Quoting from the Qur'an, 2:216, she writes: "Fighting is decreed for you, much as you dislike it." Naseef ranks jihad as next in importance to the five pillars of Islam (Naseef 1999: 152). She quotes a tradition taken from the Prophet's wife Aisha stating that although jihad for women may be "without fighting," it remains jihad. Indeed, in a case where infidels invade a Muslim country, "all the inhabitants of this country should go out and fight the enemy. In this situation, it is unlawful for anyone to refrain from fighting" (153). Further, during these exceptional times women can act without their husbands' permission, as may "the child without the father's permission, and the slave without his master's permission" (153). Individuals become responsible for working out what are the appropriate hierarchies to which they must respond. Naseef goes on to quote the Egyptian Islamist scholar Sayyid Qutb, who asserted that women may participate in jihad if absolutely necessary. Women surrounding the Prophet provided precedents (154). As we shall see, Islamic feminists like al-Ghazali and Naseef are clear on what their primary role is: wife and mother. However, the needs of jihad may interfere. Both of these women tell of Nusayba Bint al-Ka'b, who fought during the Battle of Uhud (625 C.E.), defending the Prophet vigorously. Naseef writes that "[c]ontinuous traditions have reached us relating women's participation in jihad throughout Islamic history" (155).

Islamic Feminism

Some women are joining religious groups despite their gender conservatism. Others are fighting these same groups, fearing the dangerous chemistry of politics and religion. Whether through or against religion, they are choosing to become part of the struggle for a better world. The question many pose to women who voluntarily Islamize is: Do they accept their communities' reactionary norms or do they appropriate and in the process subvert them? If there are some who can be considered "feminists" according to my definition of the term (see the introduction), how do they adapt their convictions that women have certain rights with the perceived need to subsume them to the community interest? How will the ways in which they position themselves to assert responsibility for the construction of their own, new religious "identity" change the face of Islam? How does participation in jihad allow for feminist activism? These are questions I engage in the rest of this book.

Some women have experimented with the concept of the harem, or separate women-specific space to create the conditions for empowerment, dignity, and justice for women (see for example the autobiography by Mernissi [1994]). In her 1989 film *A Door to the Sky*, the Moroccan filmmaker Farida Benlyazid explores the Islamic dimension of an all-female space. In the film, the character Nadia returns from Paris to her native Fez to be at her father's bedside as he dies. A series of unexpected encounters and experiences lead her to give up her westernized appearance and attitude and to adopt Islamic dress and norms. With a few other women, including a woman Qur'an reciter, Nadia creates a shelter for abused women out of the palace she has inherited. In their analysis of the film, Ella Shohat and Robert Stam write that life in that shelter offers "an alternative both to the Western imaginary and to an Islamic fundamentalist representation of Muslim women. Whereas contemporary documentaries show all-female gatherings as a space for resistance to patriarchy and fundamentalism, *A Door to the Sky* uses all-female spaces to point to a liberatory project based on unearthing women's history within Islam, a history that includes women's spirituality, prophecy, poetry, and intellectual creativity as well as revolt, material power, and social and political leadership" (Shohat and Stam 1994: 165). Benlyazid does not, however, advocate separatism as a long-term proposition. At the end, Nadia leaves with the man she loves and wants to marry. As a good Muslim woman she prefers to live in an integrated environment as soon as it is safe and spiritually healthy.

Separatism is not an option for those who believe in the possibility of creating the conditions in which whole individuals can live in whole societies. Some Muslim women are working within systems that marginalize them, and in the process they are becoming publicly visible and audible "in ways that were earlier unobtainable to them and on conditions they define and choose for themselves" (Ask and Tjomsland 1998: 7). Despite this unprecedented visibility, many outsiders insist on depicting these women, especially those within Islamist movements, as victims. Few are exploring what lies behind their apparent capitulations. Dutch anthropologist Wilhelmina Jansen warns against characterizing women as victims when they "take over the idiom of their oppressors and limit their freedom of dress and movement, simplify reality and exalt their domestic activities." We must try to understand their behavior beyond its surface meaning (Jansen 1998: 86). The gap between women who submit to the patriarchal rules of their chosen religious communities and those who reject such rules and norms outright may not be as great as would at first appear.

In what follows, I examine the words of a few women writers who have declared their own jihad against religious interpretations and histories that they consider to be harmful to Muslim women. Saying no to those who claim to speak for them, they are engaging in public debate about the proper roles and rights of Muslim men and women. Sometimes consciously, sometimes unconsciously, they situate themselves as *Islamic feminists*.

What do I mean when I write *Islamic feminist*? Some will protest that this identification is oxymoronic. By way of example, I shall summarize Haideh Moghissi's argument about the incompatibility between Islam and feminism, between "a religion which is based on gender hierarchy [and] the struggle for gender democracy and women's equality with men" (1999: 126). The Qur'an, for Moghissi, is unequivocally opposed to gender equality, and the "Sharia is not compatible with the principles of equality of human beings" (141). Despite its growing currency throughout the Muslim world, Moghissi asserts that Islamic feminism has no "coherent, self-identified and/or easily identifiable" ideology or movement. Those who advocate its utility as a concept and a marker for a specific brand of feminism are not women from within Muslim societies but rather "diasporic feminist academics and researchers of Muslim background living and working in the West" (126). These women she later characterizes as "exceptionally forgiving, postmodern relativist feminists in the West" whose indigenized and exotic form of Western feminism excludes "core ideas of legal and social equity, sexual democracy and women's control over their sexuality" (146). The attitudes to Islamic feminism span the gamut of leftists like herself who reject its possibility because they consider divine laws inherently hostile toward feminism, to those who "posit that feminism within an Islamic framework is the only culturally sound and effective strategy for the region's women's movement" (134). The latter group may include secularists overwhelmed by "the political and discursive influence of Islamic fundamentalism" (134). Here lies the major problem in Moghissi's argument: she confounds Islam and Islamic fundamentalism, as though the two were the same. This slippage leads her to assert that there is a general pressure today to affirm Islam, regardless of whether or not one believes in it, so as to gain credibility. This affirmation, she dramatically asserts, "relies on twisting facts or distorting realities, ignoring or hiding that which should be clear" (135). Her very real fear is that to celebrate Islamic feminism is "to highlight only one of the many forms of identity available to Middle Eastern women, obscuring ways that identity is asserted or reclaimed, overshadowing forms of struggle outside religious practices and silencing the secular voices which are still raised against the region's stifling Islamification policies" (137–38). Feminism is a secular ideology and Islam today rests on fundamentalist foundations (143). Those who advocate that feminist projects be conducted within an Islamic framework have clearly despaired of secular options for change without considering how their actions "legitimiz[e] and sanitiz[e] the political-religious dictatorship" (145).

I have elaborated Moghissi's argument against the possibility of the coexistence of Islam and feminism because it explains the anxiety many Muslim women public intellectuals, including Djebar, Mernissi, and El Saadawi, feel as they watch the Taliban taking away women's rights in Afghanistan, the Algerian Front Islamique de Salut targeting women intellectuals, the fundamentalist Sudanese goverment oppressing its women. Many are sure that compromise with such a religion is fatal. The issue I take with this attitude is not that these extremist forms of Islamic practice are benign, but rather that they are only a very small, if highly visible, part of Islam today. I would suggest that Moghissi and others skeptical of the intellectual and political viability of Islamic feminism have juxtaposed two mutually exclusive rigid ideologies, the one secular and the other fundamentalist and misogynist, and they have correctly concluded that an identity based on bringing these two incompatibles together is impossible.

Islamic feminism is not a coherent identity, but rather a contingent, contextually determined strategic self-positioning. Actions, behaviors, pieces of writing that bridge religious and gender issues in order to create conditions in which justice and freedom may prevail do not translate into a seamless identity. Indeed, Islamic feminism works in ways that may be emblematic of postcolonial women's jockeying for space and power through the construction and manipulation of apparently incompatible, contradictory identities and positions. The term "Islamic feminist" invites us to consider what it means to have a difficult double commitment: on the one hand, to a faith position, and on the other hand, to women's rights both inside the home and outside. The label Islamic feminist brings together two epithets whose juxtaposition describes the emergence of a new, complex self-positioning that celebrates multiple belongings. To call oneself an Islamic feminist is *not to describe a fixed identity but to create a new, contingent subject position.* This location confirms belonging in a religious community while allowing for activism on behalf of and with other women. This linking of apparently mutually exclusive identities can become a radical act of subversion. In the introduction to his history of identity construction in what he famously calls the Black Atlantic, Paul Gilroy writes that people who occupy the space between identities that "appear to be mutually exclusive [or who are] trying to demonstrate their continuity" are engaging in "a provocative and even oppositional act of political insubordination" (1996: 1).

Those who position themselves as Islamic feminists, even when they do not explicitly label themselves thus, may well be political insubordinates. They are refusing the boundaries others try to draw around them so as better to police them. They are claiming that Islam is not necessarily more traditional or authentic than any other identification, nor is it any more violent or patriarchal than any other religion. They are claiming their right to be strong women within this tradition, namely to be feminists without fear that they be accused of being Westernized and imitative. They are highlighting women's roles and status within their religious communities, while at the same time declaring common cause with Muslim women elsewhere who share the same objectives. They are linking their religious, political, and gender identities so as to claim simultaneous and sometimes contradictory allegiances even as they resist globalization, local nationalisms, Islamization, and the patriarchal system that pervades them all.

Islamic feminist performances and practices are situated somewhere on a continuum between the extremes of an ascribed identity of "Muslim" and an achieved identity of "Islamist." To be a Muslim is to be born into a particular religious community, to carry an identity card that checks "Muslim" next to the category "Religious Identity." Those to whom a Muslim identity is ascribed participate in a Muslim culture and community without necessarily accepting all of its norms and values. Muslims might be secular, occasionally observing some ritual, such as fasting for the month of Ramadan, while not necessarily praying regularly. Muslims might even be atheists. Islamists, on the other hand, achieve their sometimes militant identity by devoting their lives to the establishment of an Islamic state. The Islamic identification connotes another form of achieved identity, which is highly volatile and contingent. "Islamic" bridges these two poles of Muslim and Islamist identifications. It describes a particular kind of self-positioning that will then inform the speech, the action, the writing, or the way of life adopted by someone who is committed to questioning Islamic epistemology *as an expansion of their faith position and not a rejection of it.* Someone who writes a novel or a memoir as an Islamic feminist may choose another speaking position when she gives a speech or writes an essay. As we shall see in the next chapter, Zaynab al-Ghazali positioned herself as a gender-neutral Islamist in her Qur'anic exegesis (al-Ghazali 1994), but as an Islamic feminist in her prison memoirs (al-Ghazali 1986).

Whenever Muslim women offer a critique of some aspect of Islamic history or hermeneutics, and they do so with and/or on behalf of all Muslim women and their right to enjoy with men full participation in a just community, I call them Islamic feminists. This label is not rigid. It does not describe an identity, but rather an attitude and intention to seek justice and citizenship for Muslim women.

Islamic feminists like Assia Djebar, Fatima Mernissi, Nawal El Saadawi, and Zaynab al-Ghazali are learning how to take advantage of the transnationalism of Islam to empower themselves as women and as Muslims. From their multiple situations they are critiquing the global, local, and domestic institutions they consider damaging to them as women, as Muslims, and as citizens of their countries and of the world, while remaining wary of outsiders' desires to co-opt their struggle. Some are basing their activism on the outright rejection of symbols and practices they consider oppressive. Others, more subtle perhaps, are mobilizing their negative representations for positive purposes and looking to history and scripture for language, models, and agendas.

What does it mean to intercalate scripture with history as an Islamic feminist? It entails study of the life of the Prophet, of the many strong women around him, and of his founding *umma* in the seventh century, and also direct engagement with the foundational texts, rather than merely reaction to their interpretations. It involves looking at the context in which the Qur'an was revealed and these texts were written. Finally, it means applying this understanding to the present so as to question the ways in which Islamic knowledge has been produced.

Situating themselves as Islamic feminists, some are beginning to challenge conventional histories and canonical texts that either omit mention of women or stigmatize their prominence as aberration. In each case, these writers are pointing to the openness of the Qur'an and Sunna to *ijtihad*, the technical term that refers to the process of independent reasoning that scholars, but also nonscholars, may choose when a legal precedent is not immediately clear and available. As Abdullahi an-Na'im argues, Islamic rule and laws are not top-down and unchanging; they are democratic, emerging out of a community consensus that derives from individual understandings of God's laws, without privileging the identity and status of the individual interpreter. He goes on to urge advocates for women's rights to engage cultural norms and institutions when interpreting the Sharia. Why? To ensure that "their own understandings of culture prevail, rather than allow others to impose their understandings" (an-Na'im 1995: 56). Yet they must also take account of "the assumptions and methodology of traditional formulations, as well as the content of the principles and rules of *sharia*" (58). The individual and the communal are inextricably intertwined when interpreters of scripture and history seek in the past blueprints for a just future.

Some Islamic feminist interpretations focus on semantics, in particular on the meaning of equality between men and women, a bone of contention among legal scholars for centuries. Those who argue that the Qur'an advocates gender equality from the beginning of creation may quote chapter 4, verse 1, in which it is revealed that God "created you from a single being [*nafs*, a feminine word meaning soul] and created its mate of the same [kind], and spread from two many men and women." Some have even taken this verse to mean that the feminine principle is originary. Others have found confirmation for gender equality in the many verses addressed specifically to both male and female believers (*mu'minun* and *mu'minat*) or male and female Muslims (*muslimun* and *muslimat*). Islamic feminist interpreters reject the notion that equal rights, roles, and duties can be reduced to some vague notion of equal value or moral equivalence of gender-specific roles and responsibilities, lest the role of the mother be deemed equal to, indeed higher than that of the breadwinner. This they call "complementarity," a rhetorical cover for radical inequality, and a pretext to keep the honored mother in her honored home. *Qiwama* or man's assumed superiority because of the support they are expected to provide women is currently under attack.

When Manuel Castells describes the "transformation of women's work opportunities and their consciousness as undermining the legitimacy of men's domination as providers of the family" (1997: 135), he is aptly describing a hermeneutical opening for Islamic feminists. The term "providers" is arguably *qiwama*, the controversial term in Qur'an 4:34, indicating some form of domestic support enjoined upon men. Naseef interprets this verse as follows: "Men are the maintainers of women because of what Allah has given one over the other, and because they spend [to support them] from their means" (1999: 198).

Dr. Fatima is currently defining *qiwama* as maintenance and protection of the wife because she is a mother, not because she is a woman. Thus, *qiwama*, which has traditionally been viewed as the Qur'an's articulation of men's superiority, is in fact a stipulation about "responsibility and not a privilege which undermines women's rights as many have come to believe. Instead it is based on the Sharia principle of *benefits in accordance with the scale of responsibility*" (199; my emphasis). Naseef is insisting on an organic, dynamic gender-neutral reciprocity among responsibilities, duties, and rights where each remains in tension with the other two and always contingent. If I do not need support, either because I am wealthy or because I do not have children, then the legitimacy of my husband's domination is undermined. If that is the case, and the legitimacy of men's domination as providers of the family is becoming a thing of the past, then *qiwama* will lose its force in a world where reproduction technology gives women control over their bodies and allows them to understand to what extent the biological specificity of their fetus-carrying bodies forces them to be dependent on men.

Assia Djebar

Several Arab women, such as the Algerian novelist-historian Assia Djebar and the Moroccan sociologist Fatima Mernissi, have situated themselves as Islamic feminists in order to study the lives of women during the formative period of Islamic history. They have drawn on their mothers' experiences and languages, their mother tongues, to expand our understanding of the roles the founding mothers played and the status they enjoyed as individuals whom the Prophet loved, respected, and protected. Many concentrate on the period immediately following the Prophet's death in 632, because many believe it is then that the ideals began to fall apart.

Understanding the ways in which twentieth-century Arab women's participations in and contributions to the well-being of their society are almost immediately erased, some Islamic feminists are reading the past through the lens of this alarming present. They are discovering women's presence in the histories that glossed over them. They are reading in the gaps of historiography and the distortions of hermeneutics the conditions of possibility for women's agency and activism. This does not mean they believe themselves able to speak on behalf of those whose consciousness necessarily remains inaccessible, at best in the realm of speculation. Knowingly complicit with the object of their investigation, they are charting what Gayatri Chakravorty Spivak calls the subaltern subject-effect. It is not a matter of giving voice to an absence, but rather of tracking what the effect of such an absent presence must have been. The subject effect that reverberates within "an immense discontinuous network ('text' in the general sense) of strands that may be termed politics, ideology, economic history, sexuality, language, and so on" (Spivak 1987: 204). Each of these strands has its own complex of strands. There is no question of restoring what has been erased but only re-presenting its subject-effect. These Islamic feminists are constructing a countermemory that situates them between the grandmothers they are honoring and the daughters they are serving. Speaking from within this discontinuous network/text, they have collectively placed at the top of their political agenda women's right to examine the gendered formation of Islamic epistemology, but always within a global framework.

In 1991 Djebar published *Loin de Medine*, a novel-history of the seventh-century *umma*, told almost entirely by women. Energetic, intelligent, defiant of those who wanted to crush them, women used the doctrines of this new religion to empower themselves against those who would enforce pre-Islamic traditions. They exerted immense influence at the time. Djebar interweaves the classical chronicles of men like Tabari,

Ibn Hisham, and Ibn Saad with imagined verbatim accounts of three women transmitters, or *rawiyat*. Each account is between six and ten pages long. The passages told by the *rawiyat* and also the sections entitled "Voices" are in italics, as are some snippets within the other sections. The products of her imagination, these italicized voices are the subaltern subject-effects that Djebar reads back into the history that has erased their presence.

The book begins with the Yemeni queen whose husband is discovered to have retained his pagan beliefs after forced conversion to Islam. When Muhammad orders the king to be killed, his queen becomes the chief facilitator of an act designed to bring an entire nation back to Islam. She invites the murderers into the royal bedroom. The deed is done and, coincidentally, the Prophet receives divine revelation. What is the reader to make of this bloody story that pairs the beheading with a divine revelation? (Djebar 1991: 25) Does Tabari not praise the woman whose terrible deed returned a nation to the Islamic fold? Far from it! His description of her falls into a stereotype about the savagery of bedouin women, their false love, and how they use the bed of lovemaking and childbirth for slaughter. Countering Tabari, Djebar writes that this woman did for Islam what the biblical Judith did for Judaism when she decapitated Holofernes. Yet she is never described in the same laudatory terms. She is never praised for her intransigence, formidable passion, and her bravery on behalf of her people. Having saved them, she is worthy of becoming a national heroine, but does not (26). Like all the other women who played important roles in their societies, she is discredited and then disappears ignominiously out of the chronicles, her actions assigned negative meaning that no one has questioned. So why did the Prophet receive revelation at the time of this woman's intervention to save the fledgling state from relapse into apostasy? Evidence of approval of a woman's action is left ambiguous and unconnected. The deed of this early Islamic heroine survives as a trace only, a warning against women's terrifying savagery.

Djebar recreates other women leaders, including Selma, who converted so as to be liberated out of captivity, but then became an apostate and opposed the great warrior Khalid ibn al-Walid after he killed her pagan brother. Selma is viciously murdered, and Djebar wonders whether she had really been opposed to Islam (40). There were women poets, Muslims who were as equally esteemed as the men, and one unnamed member of the pagan Beni Kinda who challenged Muhammad with the power of her tongue. When he died, she turned her venom on the Muslim general Mohadjir ibn Omeyya: "You are a mere warrior. . . . My eloquence, my voice will still be there when you are dust." Incensed, he determines to deprive her not of her life but of something more valuable. He cuts out her tongue, pulls her teeth, and amputates her hands. Her response is to sing with her hands, so that her "song will remain beyond their reach." When the Caliph Abu Bakr hears the story, he is angry because he realizes that this brutal response to poetic power has given her immense moral authority (119–23).

Djebar describes the Prophet Muhammad's wives, who were important as counselors, because they were situated at the heart of the new community, not marginalized in some separate domestic space as mothers. Still today, these women serve as powerful role models. There was Khadija Bint Khuwaylid, a successful businesswoman who proposed to her employee, the future Prophet of Islam, though he was fifteen years her junior. She was the first to believe her husband when he reported his revelations in 610, and she was his first convert. When she died in 619, the Prophet Muhammad lost not only a wife but also one of his most influential supporters. Later he would marry other women, but as long as Khadija lived she was his sole partner. While every Muslim child knows that Muhammad was very close to four men who, one by one, succeeded him after his death and whose rule constitutes the golden age of the Rightly Guided Caliphs, few learn that each of these men was connected to the

Prophet by ties of marriage. Two of them, Ali and Uthman, were his sons-in-law—each married a daughter of his, Fatima and Ruqayya. The other two were his fathers-in-law—Muhammad married Aisha, the daughter of Abu Bakr, and he also married Hafsa, Umar's daughter. Like others of his wives, Aisha and Hafsa were called Mothers of the Faithful, and parts of their lives became models for the roles, responsibilities, and behaviors for future Muslim women.

Some of the Prophet's other wives remained true to Islam despite the fact that the men in their families did not convert and therefore faced punishment and even death (52). All played a part in shaping the Islamic community as we now know it. These daughters of Ishmael Djebar writes, scarcely figure in the texts of chroniclers who, however scrupulous, were "predisposed to hide women's presence." Fiction, therefore, has "to fill in the gaps in collective memory so as to locate the space and the duration of the days that I wanted to inhabit. . . . Several voices of *rawiyat* interrupt this reconstruction weaving the backdrop to this first Islamic stageset" (5). Djebar concludes her preface with the characterization of her project as "ma volonté d'*Ijtihad*" (6). In other words, this text represents her desire to engage in *ijtihad*. This self-positioning as a religious scholar authorizes this historical novelist to engage in an Islamic legal practice.

In a section devoted to Fatima, the Prophet's daughter, Djebar argues on behalf of her moral authority in Islam as a daughter, not as a wife and mother of martyrs, her usual claim to fame. When Muhammad was on his deathbed he called for a scribe to record his wishes, presumably in connection with his succession. His wives brought their fathers. Muhammad said nothing. Had Fatima been a son, Djebar surmises, Muhammad would have dictated the course the new community should take and there would not have occurred the dissension that followed (58–63). The next chapter, entitled "Voix" and formatted in the italics that mark fiction sections, plumbs Fatima's pain and inconsolable sadness at her father's death. She remains in communion with his spirit until her own death a mere six months later. Djebar is emphasizing the importance of daughters in the eyes of Muhammad. Did he not spark a revolution, what she calls the "unbearable feminist revolution" of Islam, when he made women inherit, giving daughters the right to part of their fathers' property (79)? These are the words she imagines Fatima to have said: "Muhammad is scarcely dead, yet you dare to disinherit his own daughter, the only living daugher of the Prophet himself." Accusing them of applying the law of the *jahiliya* to her, she goes to the mosque where she harangues the men for their cowardice and lethargy and warns them of God's punishment (81). She quotes Muhammad's injunctions to his people to love her.

Djebar's focus on Fatima as *daughter* turns her into Everywoman. Why? Because all women are daughters, but not all women are wives and mothers. It is as daughter, as a representative of all women, that Fatima shows women how to reject an unjust situation and to demand their rights as though they were sons, men.

Fatima was not the only woman rebel in early Islam; others also were not quietly submissive subalterns, hidden from the public eye. They were active in all spheres, including Qur'anic interpretation and the transmission of Traditions. Aisha, Muhammad's youngest wife, "The One Who Preserves the Living Word," was the one from whom the Prophet said Muslims should take half their religion. Before his death she was the one who spent the most time with him and his followers because her house was also the place of prayer. She was privy to the conversations between Muhammad and his Companions. She is said to be the first of the *rawiya* (292), and the source of over two thousand Traditions.

Djebar makes it clear that Aisha recognized the distortions the men were already introducing into the Traditions, and she assumed the responsibility to keep the record as straight as possible (300). But history did not take note because historians were inattentive to Aisha's record as an accurate transmitter of Traditions, and much too attentive to the bad stories jealous people told about her. So the history books tell us the Story of the Lie, what Djebar calls the Test, the scandal surrounding Aisha when for a month she was suspected of adultery. One day, just before her group was ready to strike camp, she went off in search of a necklace she had dropped. The caravan left without her. No one noticed her absence, since her carriers assumed that she was in her shrouded litter. As a wife of the Prophet she was expected to remain out of sight, hence her *haudaj* was always closed. In addition, she was so light that her bearers could not tell whether or not she was there. A young man found her wandering alone in the dunes and accompanied her back to her husband. Tongues wagged. For fourteen centuries, Djebar repeats, "every woman in Dar al-Islam will have to pay for the Test that lasted for a whole month of doubt. . . . The terrible doubt that will weigh heavily once, 1000 times, on each Muslim woman as soon as she takes a husband because a feather-light 14–year old girl got lost looking for her agate necklace far from the caravan . . . each husband, *volens nolens*, will revive in his wife, victim of the reingrained doubt, some of the terrible suffering of the adolescent in Medina" (288–89). What is remembered is Aisha's shame, not her pain. Another instance of unfair remembrance comes from the 656 Battle of the Camel, so named because of the camel on which Aisha sat and directed the war. What is remembered is that Aisha led the losing side. What is ignored is that she led it. In fact, this defeat gave rise to the Tradition, "Those who entrust their affairs to a woman will never know prosperity."

Fatima Mernissi

Appalled by this Tradition, Fatiwa Mernissi took up the challenge to refute it. In *The Veil and the Male Elite* (1987), she dared

to question the unquestionable, namely the reliability of a
"sound" Tradition or saying attributed to the Prophet. Such
Traditions proliferated after his death as the new Muslims
sought guidance from the Prophet's life as a model for their own.
His Companions became the authorities whose personal witness
was sufficient verification. As direct access to these Companions
dwindled and the community spread far beyond the confines of
its original Arabian heartland, new Traditions were fabricated to
respond to the changing circumstances in which Muslims found
themselves, but also—as Mernissi writes—they were introduced
for material and ideological advantage (1991: 45). It was fairly
easy to invent a saying and then attach a chain of authorities back
to a known Companion. By the ninth century there were over
half a million Traditions in circulation with no good way of
establishing the difference between those that were "sound" and
those that were "weak." A noted religious scholar named al-
Bukhari set about collecting and selecting these Traditions and
establishing rules for their verification and counterverification so
that they might be declared "sound" (*sahih*). The result was a
four-volume compilation of Traditions, *Sahih*, which has become
an unassailable source for Islamic law and norms. For twelve
centuries Muslims have been able to quote Abu Bakra's quota-
tion of Muhammad, who is supposed to have said, "Those who
entrust their affairs to a woman will never know prosperity."

Mernissi decided that if she were to question the reliability of
this misogynist Tradition, she would have to study "the religious
texts that everybody knows but no one really probes, with the
exception of the authorities on the subject: the mullahs and
imams" (2). She defiantly authorizes herself (49) to question the
claims made by people she felt she could not trust. The source of
the misogynist Tradition, a certain Abu Bakra (who is not to be
confused with the Prophet's first Caliph Abu Bakr) is the lynchpin
of its authority. Even though Abu Bakra doubtless did overhear
Muhammad say that "those who entrust their affairs to a woman

will never know prosperity," he himself has a suspect history and character. His reasons for conversion are questionable: he was a slave before becoming Muslim, and Muhammad had promised slaves manumission if they converted. Once a member of the *umma*, Abu Bakra prospered and became one of the notables in the city of Basra. When Aisha and Ali were scouting around the area in 656 looking for support in their civil war, Abu Bakra refused to commit himself to either side. When Aisha lost the Battle of the Camel, he opportunistically remembered what Muhammad had said twenty-five years earlier about the inappropriateness of the Persians choosing a woman leader. Quoting the eighth-century religious scholar Imam Malik Ibn Anas, Mernissi asserts that it is "not enough just to have lived at the time of the Prophet in order to become a source of Hadith [the Arabic word for 'Tradition']. It was also necessary to have a certain background that qualified you to speak. . . . The most important criteria were moral" (59). Yet research reveals that this was far from a moral man: the second Caliph Umar Ibn al-Khattab had ordered that Abu Bakra be flogged for false testimony!

Mernissi investigates another source of Traditions, a certain Abu Hurayra whom she found to be arrogant, stupid, and manipulative in the way he quoted the Prophet's words. As Djebar has noted, Aisha kept an eye on these men who felt free once the Prophet was dead to quote him opportunistically and even to invent words he never uttered and deeds he never performed. Few were as egregious as Abu Hurayra; several times he was recorded as having been corrected by Aisha, yet he persisted in his deviousness. Nonetheless, centuries of scholars accepted his assertion that the Prophet had said that when dogs, asses, and women intervene between the worshipper and the *qibla*, or direction of prayer toward Mecca, they disturb prayer. Mernissi's plaint is with the historians who refused, or perhaps were afraid, to acknowledge women's strong positions in

Muhammad's society, where they knew they had the right to ask how Islam "would improve their situation. This critical spirit on the part of women toward the political leader remained alive and well during the first decades of Islam. It only disappeared with the onset of absolutism . . . and the disappearance of Islam as the Prophet's experiment in living, in which equality, however merely potential it might be, opened the door to the dream of a practicing democracy" (191). Revolutionary Islam disappeared because men like Abu Bakra and Abu Hurayra willfully misrepresented Muhammad's words and actions.

Throughout, Mernissi frames her arguments and criticisms of Islamic authorities within a context of belief in the Prophet as an inspired revolutionary, a man who was opposed to violence and who envisioned a community of equals united by their spiritual bond, and not bound by tribal hierarchies (38–39). In this community "women had their place as unquestioned partners in a revolution that made the mosque an open place and the household a temple of debate" (11). The failure to perpetuate this democracy was the fault of his followers, who were still steeped in the tribal ethos and did not know how to implement his democratic, spiritually based ideas. Instead of opening up the question of succession to the community, a small elite group, "fierce with pride and drunk with the power of the bow" (10), held on to the decision-making process. Thus does Mernissi explain the violence that ensued upon Muhammad's death. For Mernissi, Islam is at once earthly and cosmological (27), sacred and material, eternal and temporal. It provides for both physical and spiritual well-being.

Moving from the life of the Prophet and the ideals he preached for a democratic revision of norms and practices, Mernissi's next project skips fourteen centuries to the post–Gulf War Arab world. Yet the concerns are the same: a beautiful, flexible, self-renewing religious core in conflict with its despotic and corrupt political superstructure, and the split between blind obedience to a misinterpreted scripture and freedom of thought within a secular Western-style democracy. Mernissi is addressing several audiences simultaneously, alternately blaming and praising Arab readers, then Muslims and then Western readers. Her admonitions seem to come from an outsider, yet they merge into pleas for unity as from an insider. With whom does she identify? She seems to identify multiply so as to choose the perspective that will advance the rhetorical goal that is always informed by the need to question misogynist norms. Just as in the seventh-century Muhammad and his followers came to liberate Arabian society from its misogyny, so enlightened Muslims may today revolutionize their societies by acknowledging the transformative role of women.

The West, now that opposition to its values is no longer a nationalist mandate, must be understood for what it is, both nemesis and model. It must be rejected but also, paradoxically, emulated. The neocolonial enemy that has harnessed time for its own nefarious purposes, it nonetheless demonstrates the effectiveness of rationalism. Creator of a global arms market that has destroyed the infrastructure of parts of the Islamic world, it nonetheless recognizes women's rights and fosters tolerance within a secular humanism. Having argued for and then against the West, Mernissi does the same in her discussion of Islam. Although it offers a "sense of identity and the power to struggle" (59), and a true understanding of Islam can become a "force for the destabilization of privilege" (113), there is a danger today that fundamentalist movements within the "New World Order," which is dependent on plentiful supplies of oil, will turn it into "tele-petro-Islam." Having condemned the Islamists, Mernissi then goes on to borrow their language: we must study the feared, violent *jahiliya*, or "age of ignorance," as the pre-Islamic era came to be known, because it is there that today's ignorance finds its roots. Like the Islamists, she advocates a renewal in the current *jahiliya*. Like them, she wants a new system, an Islamic community true to the principles of the founding community. Unlike them, she does not want an Islamic state.

Arguing for openness to pluralism as the only way to respond to the challenge of globalization that makes the "fiction of homogeneity" of the *umma* increasingly difficult to sustain, Mernissi points to the centrality of women in the debate about democracy. She shows how liberal democracies contradict their own rhetoric about the importance of "democratization, the development of civil society, and women and minority status in the community" by allying themselves with "conservative and reactionary rulers" with whom they agree about the need for stability and the elimination of conflict for the pursuit of profit. Demographic changes and the empowerment of marginalized groups has "forced both Western and Arab rulers to reconsider their strategies." As flows of migrations are being stanched, responsibility falls on both "Eastern and Western" states to "accept 'global' responsibility for promoting freedom, pluralism, gender equality, and democracy" (Mernissi 1995: 44–45). No sooner has the reader pigeonholed Mernissi as betraying one group than she attacks its enemy, positioning herself as part of that very same group. She will not be caught in the contradictions that she consciously constructs.

Nawal El Saadawi

This agility in confronting multiple audiences characterizes the writings of Nawal El Saadawi also. For Djebar, Mernissi, and El Saadawi writing is a vital weapon in the fight to establish justice within a system that "draws its authority from the autocratic power exercised by the ruler of the state, and that of the father or the husband in the family. The written word for me became an act of rebellion against injustice exercised in the name of religion, or morals, or love" (El Saadawi 1999: 292). What El Saadawi opposes is the political, ideological use of religion.

Most would be surprised at my placing El Saadawi among the ranks of Islamic feminists. Even Anne Roald, who has included the Egyptian activist among feminists engaged in reforming or reconstructing their religion, has called her a *rejectionist* (Roald 1998: 20). This label contrasts her with other women whom Roald categorizes as *loyalist, revisionist, sublimationist,* and *liberationist.* Yet for me, some of El Saadawi's writings are clearly Islamic feminist.

She has dedicated her life to investigating the relationships among domestic, local, and international sources of oppression on women and to exposing the dangers in dichotomized thinking. The devil, she wrote in an essay on dissidence and creativity (both attributes of the devil), "is responsible for disasters, defeat and misery. But the devil has no power relative to god. Though god has all the power, he is not responsible for any disaster, defeat or misery. The split between power and responsibility has lain at the core of oppression and exploitation from the advent of slavery to this day" (El Saadawi 1995: 9). The devil who has no power but who is made to shoulder responsibility for all evil is embodied in women. Therefore, their bodies are obscenities to be hidden. Having linked women with the devil, men then persecute them (1980: 46, 59). El Saadawi is not attacking Islam but the God-Satan dichotomy. Linking local and global terrorism with philosophical, cultural, and economic imperialism, she shows how indigenous cultures and religions have been used "to serve their own economic and intellectual interests" (1995: 10). Hope lies in God becoming a dissident, and then "we have to declare the innocence of the devil" (15). This, then, is the meaning of the title of a recent novel.

The Innocence of the Devil (1994) joins other Islamic feminist texts to question another foundational narrative. This one, however, is not of the Islamic but of the Abrahamic community. The story is set in a yellow pharaonic palace that has become a psychiatric hospital. Most of the patients meld into a kind of Greek chorus made up of bald men with scraggly beards and women in white. Three patients stand out. One thinks he is God. One is named Eblis (Arabic for "the devil"). The third character is Eblis's childhood friend Gannat, whose name means "paradises." Gannat was born with her eyes open and total recall. Her extraordinary memory, which goes back five thousand years to when the serpent whispered to the still-pure angel Eblis, is considered a disease and she is institutionalized (El Saadawi 1994: 210–12). The goal is to rid her of this terrible memory.

As soon as Gannat walks into the hospital she recognizes God because "he was wearing the white coat of the Director, and the body of her grandfather, and the hooked nose of Zakaria, and the square white face of the King, and the turban of Sheikh Bassiouni with the long feather standing in the air at the top" (208). In other words, God is interchangeable with all the abusive men she has known and whose violence she has experienced as incest and rape. Eblis, on the other hand, is playfully rebellious, mocking the old fool who thinks himself God, and ready to help women in ways he cannot help himself: "The Devil was known in the village since the early days of the first Pharaoh of Egypt. They had seen him walk at night close to the cemetery. He stole into the body of women much more often than men, giving them the strength of forty men" (77). This was what he did when Gannat was to be taken for electroshock treatments. He tried to protect her against their violence by locking her body to the bed, and they said that the devil had "taken over her body" (103).

Unlike God who is constantly slipping into other forms, Eblis remains himself, a source of strength. It is he who saved the pharaonic palace from collapsing (4). At the end of the novel, God declares Eblis innocent, thus destroying his own identity by becoming dissident to himself. The collapse of the God-Eblis tension reveals the vanity of trying to know God through his opposite. The God who is paired with the devil is the God of organized monotheistic religions. The God who is knowable only through his opposite is a tyrant to be resisted. El Saadawi's God is glimpsed through the effects of his essence, which is the rule of justice. We find ourselves with the God of Nawal's grandmother and of her childhood in an Egyptian village on the River Nile (El Saadawi 1993).

How can I justify calling this an Islamic feminist novel? Some may feel that the judges who condemned El Saadawi to death were right to find this novel deeply offensive, heretical even (Farahat 1993). They may not agree with the punishment, but harbor the kinds of misgivings that some did about Salman Rushdie's intentions when he wrote his *Satanic Verses* in the late 1980s. Clearly, El Saadawi is staying close to the bone, compelling her reader to pay attention to her real intent. What this reader has understood is that if women are always associated with the devil, the corollary must be that men are associating themselves with God. In a religion like Islam where God is transcendent and humans are not supposed to experience divine immanence, such a notion is blasphemous. Worse, the characters blur into each other as abusive figures of unprincipled authority, and some call themselves God so as to do anything, include rape. This cannot be God. So who or what is God? This anthropomorphized God is more like the God of established Judaism and Christianity whose images we in the West know so well. To reject this God is to open up the possibility of thinking about who God really might be. El Saadawi's writings suggest that good Muslims should accept that the God of Islam may be knowable through his revealed word only. Each individual must accept this divine word, which was materialized in the Qur'an, so that it may become the sole guide in and through life. No one has the right to tell another who God is beyond the Qur'an, nor to impose rules, roles, and rights in God's name.

In the first volume of her autobiography, entitled *Daughter of Isis*, El Saadawi states how it was that religion was made repugnant to her. In high school her religious studies teachers deliberately made the Qur'an difficult and inaccessible. They took pleasure in "choosing meanings that one's reason refused, explanations that made things more confused, in proferring threats of hell-fire, or hopes of a paradise where there was nothing to do except loll on sofas, or sleep, or eat" (El Saadawi 1999: 216). Although she did pass through a period of religious devotion later in high school, she never ceased questioning the ways in which religious authorities distorted the Qur'an and various aspects of Islam (250–52).

The other erroneous association that El Saadawi is attacking is the one often made by Muslim authorities between women's inherent evil and Eve. Gannat remembers her grandmother calling her "fallen" and exclaiming in alarm, when she was born with her eyes open, that she must be the devil and therefore she was fallen, like Eve. Shaykh Bassiouni tells Gannat that her "eyes are full of Eve's lust. . . . Some saw in them the deep sadness which was born ever since the day when Eve had sinned" (31–33). In the Qur'an, however, Eve is never mentioned, only Adam (2:37). Direct references to Eve as temptress are not Islamic but rather misogynist accretions taken from the two other religions of the Book (167). Additionally, the snippets of Qur'anic verses taken out of context—for example, to quote "men are *qawwamun* over women" without the rest of the verse that explains why (134)—and then used to insult women, form a biting critique of the ways in which some male religious authorities use the scriptures to their own ends. They can go so far as to say, "It is forbidden to speak to God. . . . God does not speak to females" (193). The Egyptian Shaykh al-Sha'rawi who condemned El Saadawi as an infidel would have no trouble agreeing! In fact, in his trial of El Saadawi he virtually said so himself (see below, chapter 5).

El Saadawi does not restrict her criticism to Islamic authorities and rhetoric, but always looks at the larger picture. In this novel, as elsewhere, she contextualizes Islam within the three monotheistic religions of the Book and their place in a largely patriarchal neocolonial system. Her simultaneous targeting of these other religions while questioning the global forces that make these men act in these ways reveals that it is these men who are the heretics and not she.

Conclusion

Situating themselves at the nexus of religion, place, transnationality, and feminist practice, Djebar, Mernissi, and El Saadawi speak with the tongues of their mothers and grandmothers to challenge traditional interpretations of authoritative texts. They deconstruct the discourses that have served to construct norms that exclude them as women. At the same time, they continue to defend their communities against detractors. They are balancing national, transnational, and feminist agendas in their attempts to construct a society hospitable to them. They thus enact Homi Bhabha's hope that new knowledge can be articulated by "the minority that resists totalization" (Bhabha 1994: 162). They are claiming multiple overlapping and sometimes contradictory allegiances while recognizing that others may ignore these plural identities and ascribe an allegiance other than the one they advance. Yet they are less susceptible to surprise ascription because of their multiple consciousness: they know who they are and how others perceive them, both from within the nation and beyond it.

A brief anecdote from Leila Ahmed's autobiography *A Border Passage* provides another illustration of how this multiple consciousness works. She relates her introduction to Western feminist theory through the writings of U.S. feminists like Kate Millett and Mary Daly, and to American feminist praxis, which is "militant, vital, tempestuous, passionate, visionary, turbulent"

(Ahmed 1999: 291). Just as the reader is about to believe that Ahmed is wholeheartedly advocating U.S. feminism, with its "raw, exhilarating energy and a sense, intellectually, of free-wheeling anarchy," she presents its underside. The Christian and Jewish feminists who were examining and rethinking their own traditions could not tolerate the same in Muslim women scholars whose "salvation entailed not arguing with and working to change our traditions but giving up our cultures, religions, and traditions and adopting theirs" (292). Praising these women for their commitment to auto-critique, she demands the same right for herself as an Islamic feminist. Ahmed was looking for that space in which she could be a self-critical American feminist while also examining and rethinking Muslim norms and values so that they might be more accommodating to women.

Intellectuals who have written Islamic feminist texts are drawing on their transnational political, religious, and gender identities in order to speak effectively to, with, and against several audiences. They are tracing the ways in which these various communities have constructed and erased them as subjects of history and hermeneutics. By holding their readers and interlocutors in tension with one another, they are complicating and undermining accusations of cultural betrayal. They are creating themselves as subjects of their own histories, but always with the understanding, as Judith Butler writes, that to remain in control they must "replay and resignify the theoretical positions that have constituted [them], working the possibilities of their convergence, and trying to take account of the possibilities that they systematically exclude." These positions are "fully embedded organizing principles of material practices and institutional arrangements, those matrices of power and discourse that produce [them] as a viable 'subject'" (Butler 1995: 42). Relocating the knowledges that were produced about them and served to exclude them, they are pointing to what fills those spaces left empty by official histories. When public intellectuals situate themselves as Islamic feminists, they address themselves to dominant religious discourses. It is from official historiography and hermeneutics that they derive their strategies to construct a feminist position that resists exclusion and locates authority within the same cultural boundaries.

4

A Muslim Sister

The best-selling prison memoirs *Days from My Life* by the Islamist leader Zaynab al-Ghazali provide a fascinating contrast and complement to the Islamic feminist texts discussed in the previous chapter. Imprisoned for her part in the 1960s Muslim Brothers' alleged conspiracy to kill the Egyptian president, Gamal Abd al-Nasir (Nasser), she narrates the miracles she performs as she endures torture. In the language of Sufi saints, she describes her journey into the heart of hell and out again. Throughout she contrasts her superior vision and spiritual power and influence with those of the Muslim Brothers, who crumbled under pressure. She describes herself as admonishing the Brothers for their lack of spirituality. Yet, even as she presents her own behavior as exemplary for all Muslims because of its unswerving commitment to Islam and the establishment of the Islamic state, she continues to insist that the first duty of the Muslim woman is to be wife and mother. Only then, when she has satisfactorily fulfilled these duties, can she contemplate other activities. Yet she, Zaynab al-Ghazali, has dedicated her life to serving God, a dedication that sometimes stands in the way of her earthly, womanly duties. Thus does al-Ghazali guide her numerous women readers to an almost unthinkable compromise between domesticity and political activism.

Is she an Islamic feminist? Few have described her as such, yet with other Islamic feminists like Assia Djebar and Fatima Mernissi, she is engaging in Islamic discourse in a way that is empowering for herself as well as for those who read her life as a model for their own. She tells the story of her leadership of the Muslim Ladies' Association, of her dealings with leading members of the fundamentalist Muslim Brothers, who were outlawed in 1948, conspired with the nationalists in 1952, and were again suppressed by the very nationalists they had helped to bring to power; of her opposition to Nasser in the 1950s and 1960s; of the banning of her association in 1964; of her arrest in 1965; and of her consequent six years spent first in the War Prison and then in Qanatir, the women's prison in Cairo.

Zaynab al-Ghazali introduces her exemplary tale of imprisonment and enlightenment, her "*legend* of torture and hardship" (al-Ghazali 1986: 86; my emphasis), with a formula that prefaces all Sufi tracts: "Prayers and peace on our master, Muhammad, and on his family and on his companions." The initiated reader expects a spiritual text. Then, after suspension dots, she declares her jihad, couched in the terms of the autobiographical pact: "The thought of writing about days from my life challenged me and I was very hesitant. However, many of those whose faith in the Islamic cause I trust—my sons, my brothers, pioneers in *da'wa* [Arabic for 'religious mission'] and the builders of its concept who lived that time with me—considered that it was a rightful duty to Islam that we record this period during which the Islamic *da'wa* struggled against the forces of heresy and evil in the East and in the West" (5). She and those close to her in her jihad consider her experiences to be public property, important enough that they should become instructive for others.

Like all women's autobiographies and especially prison narratives—for example, El Saadawi's *Memoirs from the Women's Prison* (1983)—*Days from My Life* presents itself as a coherent articulation of a politicized self in relationship with a society that it may then transform. It affirms the importance of a woman's life, especially after she has suffered as a political prisoner (Harlow 1992: 133–48). Whereas El Saadawi was immediately sent to Qanatir, the women's prison, al-Ghazali was not sent there until she had first spent a year in the War Prison with men like the famous religious leader and ideologue Sayyid Qutb as well as thousands of other Muslim Brothers. She can, therefore, from the start compare herself with men, put herself on a par with them, often even place herself above them. This personal memoir is a political text written by a woman who understands what it means for a woman to write her life.

Days from My Life does not appear in a political vacuum. It is a genre piece that recalls comparable experiences that Muslim Brothers who had been imprisoned in the 1950s and 1960s described in their memoirs. Gilles Kepel writes that the martyrology of the Nasser period was of "the utmost importance for the subsequent Islamicist movement. The halo of persecution suffered in defense of a faith and a social ideal confers a status of absolute truth upon Islamicist discourse" (Kepel 1985: 25). To write one's memoirs was not a self-centered indulgence, but rather constituted an act of guidance for others. In his analysis of this text as one example among others of Islamist resistance discourse, Timothy Mitchell has written that they demonstrated "how to answer the accusations of the regime in the idiom of Islam . . . the description of prison life becomes a detailed diagnosis of the state's methods of control. Thus such memoirs can themselves show how these methods actually participate in producing the political discourse of Islam . . . these forms of opposition were not something external to the system of power but the product of techniques and tensions within it" (Mitchell 1988: 3, 6, 9). In addition to providing guidance for others similarly situated, these memoirs enact a model for Islamic feminism, but always within the religious framework of a well-understood and interpreted Islam.

Zaynab al-Ghazali's Muslim Ladies' Association

In 1935, at the age of eighteen, al-Ghazali dedicated her life to Islam. For a year she had been a member of the Egyptian Feminist Union that Huda Shaarawi had founded in the 1920s. Soon, however, she became disaffected, and she broke away to form an association for pious Muslim women apparently concerned less with women's liberation than with social welfare and Islamic education projects. It was not so much that she was embracing traditional, patriarchal values, but rather that, like other Islamic feminists, she was resisting what she considered to be the Western bias of the Egyptian Feminist Union, which had "wanted to establish the civilisation of the Western woman in Egypt and the rest of the Arab and Islamic worlds." She used a rhetorical device common to nineteenth- and early-twentieth-century Arab women's polemical treatises: negative comparisons with Western women were deliberately made up front so as to enable the author to shoot down criticisms. The argument was always, "We want to be educated for the sake of our sons, the next generation of men, and not so as to become equal with our husbands. We are not like European women, whose goal is the destruction of their family and by extension of their society."

As the daughter of an Azhar-trained cotton merchant, al-Ghazali had wished to retain a more Islamic orientation as she sought social justice for women and men alike and equality between them. Indeed, she sometimes cooperated with secular feminists when nationalist causes were at stake. For instance, in 1952 al-Ghazali and her association joined the Women's Committee for Popular Resistance in their support of the male nationalists in the independence struggle (Badran 1991: 210, 213).

A careful reading of her management and direction of the Muslim Ladies' Association supports the contention that she never abandoned but rather refocused her feminist aspirations. Although she often advocates strict adherence to scriptural norms of proper conduct for women—modesty, maternity, and attention to the well-being of the home—al-Ghazali in the same breath describes a life, her own, dedicated to a jihad to convert the Egyptian people and their government to true Islam. She claims that her religiopolitical goals necessitate for her, as they should for any God-fearing Muslim woman, changes in expectations for ideal peacetime behavior; she describes herself as compelled to set aside domestic duties so as to free herself up to fight the jihad that will establish the Islamic state that recognizes men and women as equal.

Jihad is not male-specific, but rather is an activity that includes women. Al-Ghazali's heroines are the early Muslim "women warriors, including Layla bint Tarif, a member of the extremist Kharijite sect that was largely obliterated in warfare with the larger Muslim community, and the woman who inspired her in her youth, and Nusayba bint Ka'b al-Maziniyya who fought with the Prophet at the battle of Uhud" (Hoffman 1995: 216), as well as the Prophet's women companions. She describes how one of these women "sacrificed herself, her husband, and her children while the male companion sacrificed only himself" (Badran 1991: 226). She calls herself a "'soldier' in the common struggle for the creation of an Islamic state" (Hoffman 1995: 213). This use of the term "soldier" reveals al-Ghazali's understanding of her role in the modern age, or new *jahiliya* (originally the name applied to the age of ignorance that preceded Islam). To recognize this twentieth-century *jahiliya* entails joining the jihad and becoming a soldier for God. As mentioned in chapter 3, for women to become jihad soldiers meant improvising new rules of conduct. These rules for military men often contravene peacetime norms; for example, in war to kill is not to murder but to be a hero (see cooke 1997). In al-Ghazali's case, these new rules might not be as lethally paradoxical, but they could be as radically transformed.

Days from My Life traces out a path that reconciles apparently contradictory prescriptions for Muslim women as opposed to Muslim soldiers by making them mutually inclusive. The ideal Muslim woman must work out, with God's help, priorities for her life: Should she stay in the kitchen or should she go out into the battlefield? The true believer will not be confused, nothing is more important than building the Islamic state. From the beginning, al-Ghazali conceived of the Muslim Ladies' Association as equal and equivalent to, yet deliberately separate from, that of the Muslim Brothers. When Hasan al-Banna', the leader of the Brotherhood, invited her to incorporate her association into his, she refused. However, and as was the case in her dealings with the secular feminists during the independence struggle, autonomy did not preclude cooperation. She worked closely with leaders of the Brotherhood in an attempt to spread Islamic education throughout Egypt and beyond. Her insistence on segregation allowed her to hold on to her power base. She must have feared that had she accepted alliance any notion of equality would have degenerated into complementarity at best, subordination at worst. It was not until the late 1940s, when the government dissolved their formal organization and just before Hasan al-Banna's assassination, that she allowed her association to come under the aegis of the Brotherhood.

The leader of the Muslim Ladies' Association knew full well and often publicly articulated Islamic stipulations for Muslims in general as well as for Muslim women in particular: marriage. Since there is no priesthood, there can be no spiritual hierarchy predicated on degrees of celibacy. The Muslim devotee or saint should not have a radically different life from the ordinary Muslim. Unlike Christian saints, who are expected to be both celibate and chaste, Muslim saints are expected to have a normal family life (Schimmel 1982: 150). While the fourteenth-century Margery Kempe had to justify being married to a man as symbolic of her real marriage to God, the Muslim woman saint has to explain why she is *not* married (Ross 1991: 527–46). This is what the eighth-century Sufi saint Rabi'a al-'Adawiya had to do. When the Sufi Hasan al-Basri proposed to her, Rabi'a is supposed to have said, "The ties of marriage apply to those who have being. Here being has disappeared for I have become nought to self and exist only through Him. I belong wholly to Him. I live in the shadow of His control. You must ask my hand of Him, not me" (Arberry 1966: 46).

If all Muslims must marry and Muslim women must make marriage their first priority, how can the Muslim woman become politically active without jeopardizing her Islamic credentials? In a 1981 interview, al-Ghazali is explicit about the connections between marriage and *da'wa:*

The Brotherhood considers women a fundamental part of the Islamic call. They are the ones who are most active because men have to work. They are the ones who build the kind of men that we need to fill the ranks of the Islamic call. So women must be well educated, cultured, knowing the precepts of the Koran and Sunna, knowing world politics, why we are backward, why we don't have technology. The Muslim woman must study all these things, and then raise her son in the conviction that he must possess the scientific tools of the age, and at the same time he must understand Islam, politics, geography, and current events. . . . Islam does not forbid women to actively participate in public life . . . *as long as that does not interfere with her first duty as a mother, the one who first trains her children in the Islamic call. So her first, holy, and most important mission is to be a mother and wife. She cannot ignore this priority.* If she then finds she has free time, she may participate in public activities. . . . Marriage is a sure Sunna . . . a mission and a trust in Islam. Sexual life in Islam is a necessity for both men and women, but it is not the first and last goal of marriage. (Hoffman 1985: 236–37; my emphasis)

In a 1981 editorial al-Ghazali wrote for the women's section of *Al-Da'wa* magazine, she emphasizes again women's domestic duties to the extent of describing work outside the home as "contrary to a woman's nature. . . . The family comes first. If an urgent need arises, then work in education until you marry; then work stops, except in absolute necessity. . . . Return, my dear, to the house. Stay in your home and obey your husband. You will be rewarded for your obedience to your Prophet and to him" (Hoffman 1995: 216).

First of all, she emphasizes women's political centrality to *da'wa*. This would seem to be a feminist move, however she couches her argument in conservative terms; her plea for the politicization of women contains no apparent threat. It is through domestic roles, she asserts reassuringly, that women gain access to the world of politics, of men. Women must be educated not to challenge men in the workplace, but rather so that they may educate their sons (note that she does not plead for women's education on behalf of the next generation, and certainly not on behalf of their daughters). So, political engagement is to work behind the scenes, to be the power behind the throne? Not quite. Albeit negatively, she declares that Islam gives women the right to become actively engaged in public life. Having first blurred the border between private and public domains through her discussion of the purpose of women's education—that is, to be effective mothers in the home to future generations of public men—she seems to go on to eliminate ambiguity. Islam welcomes women into public space, but only after they have been good wives and mothers in the private space. The nervous man who may have balked at the implication that women might be trespassing on his turf is reassured.

However, upon closer scrutiny, it appears that this comfortable dichotomizing is in fact illusory, if not outright fallacious, since the logic of her argument strongly suggests that public action represents the culmination of private activities. These are not separate realms but rather behaviors ranging across a continuous spectrum. To be a wife and a mother in Islam entails a religious, political activism that cannot be confined to the home, even if that is where it starts. So what of efficient wives and mothers who can manage their time so as to accomodate spells of *da'wa* in their spare time? Or of women like Zaynab al-Ghazali, who have no children and only tamed husbands? They must throw themselves wholeheartedly into political action, for it is only thus that they can obey the demands of a well-understood Islam. Zaynab al-Ghazali intimates that all Muslims, including women, must free themselves from the constraints imposed by a poorly understood Islam, become active and engage in jihad to establish an Islamic state. It is this Islamic state that provides a loophole for women's activism and public agency.

Survival in Hell

Days of My Life skims over the early years to home in on al-Ghazali's first year of imprisonment in the men's War Prison. This year is the spiritual high point of her life. Almost as though she were describing another person's experience, she details the terrible things the Egyptian authorities do to her because of her alleged collusion in a plot to assassinate the president. She sets herself up as the rightly guided, strong victim whose body submits without complaint to unspeakable pain.

She may not call her months in the War Prison a journey, yet the stages through which al-Ghazali passes do suggest mystical movement. First, there is the descent, and at the end, ascent, but in between there is horizontal, circular movement. There is little sense of the usual linear progression inherent in the spiritual journey. Rather, the journey seems to consist of a movement through concentric circles that ripple out from the still center that is Zaynab. Torture and pain drag her out of her center to touch others. Yet each touch anchors her more firmly in herself and strengthens her ability to ripple out again for the sake of others.

This extended parable of the struggle by the devil to wrest al-Ghazali's soul out of its safekeeping in God's hands chronicles a woman's descent into hell, the purification through torture and the reascent to earth to minister to the world. This is the ultimate test: to pass through hell unweakened in spirit and belief. Zaynab's body becomes the battlefield on which the contest between good and evil is played out. The War Prison is called a "hell that was a crucible for the melting of men's metals" (7), but perhaps not of women's metal, and certainly not of Zaynab. The jailors and the torturers are repeatedly called *zabaniya*, or the angels who guard the gates of Hell (Qur'an 74:30). They inflict unbearable tortures, but she is so miraculously able to endure that even a jailor cannot stop himself from asking whether she might not consider herself, or in fact be, a *qiddisa* (Arabic for a Christian saint; the Muslim saint is a *wali*). She writes, "Riyad entered the cell slowly, carefully. His face betrayed an amazement he tried to hide with conceit: 'So, you want to be a *qiddisa?* . . . You want them to build a tomb for you in a mosque 30 years after your death and to say that Zaynab al-Ghazali al-Jabili performed miracles in the War Prison?'" (al-Ghazali 1986: 104–5)

For the prison authorities, writes al-Ghazali, Nasser is God whose name is invoked before speaking just as Muslims invoke God's name before performing any action: "I say to you in the name of Gamal Abd al-Nasir" (69). She is told, "If you say Lord, no one will save you. But if you say Nasser, then Paradise, Nasser's Paradise, will open up to you" (94); "Where is your Lord? Call on him to save you from me. . . . Call for Nasser and you'll see what'll happen" (91). Through prison intermediaries Nasser offers her the world, which includes support for her association and its magazine and even the post of minister of social affairs, in exchange for her recognition of Nasser as the ultimate authority in her life. Without weighing the consequences, she contemptuously rejects all such temptations.

She suffers seven kinds of torture, each associated with a separate cell, a separate hell: (1) whippings, as many as 1,000 per session; (2) attack dogs and men, but whereas the dogs bite and tear at her flesh, the men never manage to rape her; (3) up to weeklong immersion in water; (4) rats; (5) hanging and whipping; (6) fire, out of which she, like Abraham and numerous martyrs before her, emerges unsinged; (7) hanging by her arms from two rings attached high to poles until she drops and then is suspended again. In a manner remarkably reminiscent of hagiographies that rarely if ever allow any but human agents to destroy the saint, al-Ghazali shows that fire and beasts are ineffective—humans must bear sole responsibility for the destruction of God's creature (Brock and Harvey 1987: 18).

The memoirs from the time she enters prison are almost formulaic, focusing surreally on recurrent statements and events, notably the call to prayer five times a day. At first, with the help of Qur'anic recitations, she miraculously withstands the whips and dogs. Eventually, however, she is taken to the prison hospital, where she often returns since the jailors try to break her without killing her. Like torturers of Christian martyrs, their goal was to restructure "a society . . . isolation is to provide a setting in which the torturer can remake the unsupported victim into a compliant citizen. . . . Thus the torturer's most effective way to deconstruct the victim's world is through the body's sensing, integrative, and expressive abilities" (Tilley 1991: 468–69). The Egyptian authorities want to eliminate al-Ghazali's countervision and to remake her in their own image.

They did not reckon on her resistance. Her survival, she writes with pride, strikes awe even in the hearts of the *zabaniya,* some of whom reaffirm their faith. In spite of herself al-Ghazali is allowed to continue to perform *da'wa* even in the heart of hell. Such a description of the spiritual awakening of evil ones is clearly designed to provide powerful testimony not only to the conversionary power of her actions and sheer endurance but also to her recognition of the potential good latent in the hearts of the apparently irredeemable. Of this event she writes, "My brother reader, I shall tell you a story about something that happened to me when I was in hospital that will make you more certain that these people are basically good and that their hearts are pure" (1986: 70). After converting Salah, she sends him for religious instruction to Sayyid Qutb, the Islamist leader, theologian, and ideologue, who is in a nearby cell. She presents herself as the agent of conversion, while others will continue the task in whatever way they deem to be necessary and appropriate. However corrupt the world, it remains susceptible to the good works of the rightly guided. Muslim women and men, particularly the specially chosen, have a single duty, and that is to work in the world until it is ready for the establishment of the Islamic state.

Signs Taken for Wonders

Her steadfastness is conveyed as being supported and rewarded by the Prophet Muhammad himself. Even the narrative structure of *Days from My Life* reinforces this relationship: the seven chapters of the book echo the seven differently numbered cells through which she passes; these cells/hells can be seen to be the obverse of the seven heavens through which Muhammad passed on the *mi'raj*, or his Ascension to meet with God. This then becomes the model of the saint's journey. Hagiographers represent the course of saints' lives "as inevitably leading up to the particular religious or philosophical choice he has made; the central experience of conversion is retold in a way which accords with the account of the life as a whole, rather than as it actually happened" (Kilpatrick 1991: 2). Al-Ghazali's journey seems rather to be the reverse: being chosen as enemy number one of Nasser, the false god; descending into the hell of prison; exhibiting patience in the face of temptations and unbearable physical testing; without guidance revealing spiritual knowledge; repeating again and again that she and hers will establish an Islamic state; performing *da'wa* in hell in anticipation of the reascent and prosecution of *da'wa* on earth. Torture for al-Ghazali was a means to her goal of salvation, but it was above all a lesson and a guide for others. Her sufferings seem to be less felt than they are presented as spectacle. Her divinely protected body becomes the instrumentality through which others may be saved.

On the journey, she is vouchsafed three visions. In the first vision, which she has during the first few days of her time in the War Prison, she sees herself at the end of a caravan in the desert standing behind a huge man who turns out to be none other than

Muhammad. Five times she asks him if he is indeed Muhammad, always prefacing her question with the Sufi invocation "*ya habibi*," meaning "my darling." Each time, he responds that he is and that she is on the path to the truth. The intimacy of their communion is underscored by his once calling her "*ya ghazali*," meaning "my gazelle." This vision establishes reciprocity of intimacy between her and Muhammad, each addressing the other using the first person possessive pronoun. The association with the gazelle, the symbol of the beloved, added to Zaynab's astonishment at being called by her generally unknown birth certificate name, Ghazali, rather than by the common misnomer *al*-Ghazali, emphasizes the significance of this appellation (50).

The next two visions constitute evidence that she has reached the highest level in faith and works, so that she is comparable both with Hasan al-Hudaybi, who succeeded Hasan al-Banna as leader of the Muslim Brothers, and with the Prophet's wife Aisha. Her iterations of these experiences constantly serve to reinforce her worthiness of the mission that has been thrust upon her. Her visions provide further proof that she is specially chosen.

The only fellow prisoners with whom she relates are women. They are sisters, or perhaps daughters, along the road to the truth. Her last two visions of Muhammad include only women and Hasan al-Hudaybi. In the second vision, she describes herself as climbing a path up a mountain. On her way, she meets only women: Amina and Hamida Qutb, Khalida and Aliya al-Hudaybi, and Fatima Issa. She asks each one if she is on "the path," and each replies that she is. *She meets no men on the road.*

At the top of the mountain is a stretch of ground on which are carpets and couches and al-Hudaybi. She conveys greetings from the Prophet. Next, she sees a train pass by at the foot of the mountain. In it are two naked women. She draws al-Hudaybi's attention to these women. Surprisingly, he remonstrates that she should not concern herself with these women, to whom she is clearly opposed and with whom she is implicitly contrasted. Is she not with him at the top of the mountain and have they not both earned this position through works and blessings? Zaynab retorts that they must "oppose them until we reform them" (174). She is at the top of the mountain not only equal to the leader but is also his teacher. He would have been happy to let the world continue in its corrupt ways. He did not feel obliged to do anything for these women who represent the evils of the lower self that he had long ago left behind. This woman's chastisement of a man supposed to be superior to her is quite common in the history of Sufi women.

She is more aware than Hasan al-Hudaybi because of her sufferings and her experiences in the prison. She knows that there is no one, however apparently evil, who is impervious to the ministrations of the good. She knows that *da'wa* demands that they continue the fight until they have put the world to rights and established the Islamic state on earth. In her last vision of Muhammad, she again situates herself with women. This time it is Aisha and her female attendants. The Prophet Muhammad is with al-Hudaybi, and he keeps telling Aisha to be patient, and she in turn keeps pressing Zaynab's hand and urging her likewise to be patient (189).

Whereas women in life and women in visions provide encouragement, men provide the opportunity for favorable comparison. Any assumption that she as a woman is being treated more gently than the male prisoners is quickly dispelled by the remembrance of vivid scenes of breathless violence enacted on her body. Her ordeal persists through her obstinate refusal to comply. Even the "god of hell," Nasser, acknowledges her special suffering in gendered terms: "Zaynab al-Ghazali has suffered more than the men have suffered" (84). The torturers repeatedly assure her that all of her associates, mostly Muslim Brothers, have confessed not only their own guilt but also hers. When young Brothers are brought to her and are questioned about their relationship to her, they admit that under the lashes of the whips they would have said anything. She protests that she does not blame them, asserting that it is after all only human to break. She, however, never breaks, despite the fact that her tortures make those of all the others pale. With less apparent kindness and tolerance, she denounces all those corrupt men in official positions who use their power to control, humiliate, and abuse those under them. She denounces those husbands of Muslim Sisters who ran away when their wives were arrested (66). She damns with faint praise her own husband, who had done what he could to hold on to a wife who tolerated him at best. The circumstances surrounding his death are illuminating: when she heard of her twenty-five-year sentence, she immediately told him to sign the divorce papers so as not to have to wait. After at first refusing, he acquiesced because the government had intervened with a choice: sign the divorce papers or go to prison. Being too old and sick to risk the hardships of prison, he signed. Within two weeks he died. Without elaboration, al-Ghazali mentions that her sister had announced that he had died without honor. Implicitly she concurs with the declaration.

Having successfully shown that the men are not strong enough to fight the jihad that the world's current pitiful state requires, al-Ghazali presents herself as the ideal *mujahida* (fighter). She is like her famous forebear, Zaynab, the grand-daughter of the Prophet, who has come down to us as the model of the woman who fights alongside men in the battlefield. She is divinely prepared for her special ordeal. Her purity is so great that attempts to derail it must always fail. Her life is that of an exemplar—more importantly, of an exemplary woman. She presents herself as the sacrifice that can redeem sinning Muslims. Whereas others do not recognize that they are in hell, she is able to demonstrate through her journey into the Inferno what the forces are that the less enlightened constantly confront and that alone they cannot overcome. Even the Muslim Brothers, whose commitment to God and to the founding of the Islamic state on earth is known, were broken by the authorities. She alone was able to prevail over the enemies of her people.

Moving to the women's prison in Qanatir dampens her spirits and provides an odd twist at the end. Whereas in the War Prison she had had to face men alone, she is now surrounded by a "lost troop of wandering humanity in the depths of ignorance [who have] forgotten their humanity, purity, chastity and nobility and become animals" (195). Ironically, when in 1981 Nawal El Saadawi was thrown into that same prison, she found herself with Safinaz Qazim, a leading member of an Islamist group, and some *munaqqabat* (women wearing the distinctive veil of the fundamentalist movement)—in other words, with some Muslim Sisters like Zaynab al-Ghazali (Harlow 1992: 131). El Saadawi describes them as mostly ignorant, blindly following Islamic dictates. This secular feminist is as shocked by the Islamist women with whom she is incarcerated as is al-Ghazali when she is thrown in with secular women prisoners. These descriptions throw into question Harlow's contention that women prisoners like El Saadawi and al-Ghazali discovered their "common lot with fellow prisoners and in [their] diary rewrite the social order to include a vision of new relational possibilities which transgress ethnic, class, and racial divisions as well as family ties" (Harlow 1987: 142). This inability to empathize with their fellow women prisoners may detract from the feminist nature of their testimonies, but it also demonstrates the ways in which alliances can and cannot be made. In a prison cell, women may be less interested in founding a sisterhood than in surviving to tell the tale.

An Islamic Feminist Mission

Days from My Life is framed more as a quest narrative than as an autobiography, yet nothing is sought. Whereas most spiritual journeys involve the individual in a search, in initiation or transformation or conversion and in continuing enlightenment after learning and apprenticeship, these prison memoirs do not once dwell on what, if anything, is being learned. It refuses to engage with the subjectivity of the narrator either as spiritual seeker or as political agent. This is not the story of a personality; it is what Lejeune has called "a discourse on the self," yet, unlike most autobiographies, it does not answer the question "Who am I?" with a "narrative that tells 'how I became who I am'" (Lejeune 1989: 124). From the beginning, al-Ghazali presents herself as a powerful, already enlightened Muslim with complete knowledge who has a spiritual calling that others recognize as important for them to know. When she came out of prison, her "sons and brothers, the pioneers in *da'wa*," persuaded her of the importance of recording her experiences (5).

Days from My Life presents al-Ghazali's life mission to a corrupt Egyptian society. Although the entire book is about the remembering of pain, it indicates little if any of the anguish commonly evoked by torture victims at the impossibility of expressing the experience of violence. It is rather the triumphant recounting of *the effects such experiences have on others*. Zaynab al-Ghazali is not writing this book for herself but as a guide for others, and that is why she so often addresses her reader. Although her experiences extend over a protracted period, the narrator presents a synchronic account of the totality of those experiences. She is at all times a complete and perfect exemplar whose vocation is proven by her special relationship with the Prophet Muhammad.

Does the life she has authored conform with Islamic norms of femininity? Can she be even only close to perfect if she enjoins domesticity on pious Muslim women, yet herself controls and ignores her husband, eschews motherhood, and throws herself into the fray of worldly power and politics? Like other Arab women writers, she has written about an individual struggle for freedom and agency, even as she balances ideological commitment with what appears to be behavioral alternatives. She declares that women should marry, be obedient to their husbands, and have children. Yet she had divorced her first husband for interfering in her religious work, and agreed to remarry only under the condition that her second husband, an older man who was already married and therefore less demanding, recognize that her *da'wa* supersedes her marriage.

Before accepting his proposal for marriage, she had said to her prospective second husband:

> I have sworn an oath of fealty to Hasan al-Banna that I shall die in God's path. . . . I had decided to eliminate the question of marriage from my life so as to devote myself fully to *da'wa*. I cannot ask you today to share this *jihad*, but I can demand that you not block it. On the day that responsibility puts me in the ranks of the *mujahidin* [jihad soldiers], do not ask me what I am doing. Let the trust between us be complete; the trust between a man who wants to marry a woman who at 18 dedicated herself to *jihad* in the path of God and to the establishment of the Islamic state. And if ever the welfare of the marriage conflicts with God's *da'wa*, then the marriage shall end and the *da'wa* shall become my whole being. . . . I know that it is your right to command me and that it is my duty to obey you, but God in our souls is greater than our souls, and his *da'wa* is dearer to us than ourselves. (34–35)

She seems to be saying that she would like to obey him, but must obey God first. Her behavior is not without precedent, but rather recalls that of Sukayna (d. 671), the Prophet Muhammad's great-granddaughter through Fatima and Husayn who married five husbands, none of whom she promised to obey. Fatima Mernissi writes that in her marriage contracts, Sukayna "stipulated that she would not obey her husband, but would do as she pleased, and that she did not acknowledge that her husband had the right to practice polygamy" (1991: 192).

Accordingly, al-Ghazali's husband never asks her about her activities. Even when young men come in the middle of the night he lets them in, arranges for food and drink to be sent to her chambers, and then tells her that some of her "children" have come (al-Ghazali 1986: 35). By assigning her the role of "mother to the faithful" he defuses the tension inherent in such a meeting. As for biological children, they are so far removed from any of her priorities that in the book she does not even mention their lack. But she does not choose *against* them. In an interview, she says that she was able to devote herself to the Islamic cause because of "a great blessing, which would not usually be considered a blessing, that I never had any children." She added that because her husband practiced polygamy and was wealthy and they had servants, she was free to do what she liked while he was with his other wives (Hoffman 1995: 216). She contents herself with adopting protégés whom she calls her children.

The ideal of women's domesticity—the domain of men's rights over their female relatives—will be reconsidered when the Islamic state is built. Al-Ghazali says, "It may take generations for Islam to rule. We are not rushing ahead of ourselves. On the day that Islam rules, Muslim women will find themselves in their natural kingdom, educating men" (1986: 144). When Islam rules it will be the women who will be educating the men. In the meantime, all men and, most significantly, all women must wage a jihad whose importance overrides all other injunctions.

Zaynab al-Ghazali's life and writings propose an agenda that allows for women's empowerment beyond the home. She foregrounds the importance of women's activism in the current *jahiliya*. By her own example, she emphasizes that women should be active in seeking to apply duties to God and the Islamic state above rights of individuals. This hierarchy allows her to use the Islamic legal system to empower herself. Not only did she know that she might dictate her conditions for marriage and write them into the contract, she also turned to the "sixth" pillar of

Islam, jihad. The Islamic nation is together engaged in jihad, a war, to build the Islamic state. Hence, Muslims are subject to the abnormal rules of war that allow for the adjustment of codes of social conduct and gender arrangements in anticipation of the utopian postbellum society.

From within the Islamist movement, she advocates radical reform in power relations. To speak and to be effective, she must embrace those religiously sanctioned gender norms, all the while showing them to be contingent upon social and religious exigencies. She is like postcolonial women fighters throughout the Arab world who have "enlarged or extended their traditional roles rather than adopting a completely new one" (Giacaman and Johnson 1989: 161). She uses the rhetoric of domesticity while subverting its meaning through her behavior. If in exceptional times such as war or jihad women may relate to their husbands and children as men have always related to their wives and children, it may eventually be all right for this state of affairs to continue. Then, as in times of war, domestic roles may "become a source of resistance because women [will have] transformed their family responsibilities to encompass the entire community" (161).

Conclusion

Days from My Life offers itself as a standard of behavior and of resistance within the vision of an ideal society. Participation in jihad turns al-Ghazali into a public emblem, a model for other women who are trying to empower themselves within the framework of a well-understood Islam. She may claim in interviews and write in Islamic journals that women should restrict themselves to the home, but in her life, and significantly, in writing her life, she marginalizes domesticity and glorifies political activism. She asserts her independence by establishing a disjuncture between her words and her actions. She speaks in piously

normative terms and then proceeds to act expediently and sometimes even in contravention of what she has just said. She
explains that such exceptionality becomes mandatory when
Islamic norms and values are well understood and they are redi-
rected toward building the Islamic state. Are we to believe the
prescriptive articles for domestic others or the descriptive self-
authoring by a Muslim woman soldier? Perhaps we should
believe both at the same time.

Zaynab al-Ghazali may have been an anomaly when she wrote
her prison memoirs back in the late 1970s, but she is no longer.
Women in Islamist groups everywhere are now using her language of accommodation and resistance with no sense of contradiction. Swedish sociologist Soroya Duval writes that women
members of the Egyptian Muslim Brothers, or *Ikhwan
Muslimun*, "see it as the duty of devoted Muslims to change the
society around them into a more just and egalitarian form that
matches Islamic perceptions." How does that work? Duval
quotes an Islamist woman leader: "It is our duty as Muslim
women to have a say in the politics of our country and the politics that shape our lives as women. Politics is not only the realm
of men, as many men want to propagate. On the contrary, it has
been made our primary concern throughout Islamic history
since 1500 years ago, when the women gave the Prophet their
vote (*Baiya*) personally. We were equally addressed, and were
equal partners in matters of the state" (Duval 1998: 58). Another
Islamist woman harked back to the days of the *umma* when
women were expected to do what the men did, for no man "has
the right to deprive a woman from her Islamic mission.
Submissiveness is only to God and not to any human being. . . .
A Muslim woman should fight for her rights, even if this means
in some cases divorce" (62). The echoes from al-Ghazali ring
loud and clear!

Indeed, Duval hails al-Ghazali as a pioneer of the kind of feminism that Islamist women can espouse. She "campaigned for

women and the nation in Islamist terms, whereas the other feminists at the time campaigned for women's rights and human rights in the language of secularism and democracy. Whereas these feminists consistently stressed the superiority of the West in their feminist goals and actions, Al-Ghazali was committed to indigenous culture and to pursuing feminism in indigenous terms. She was determined to find feminism within Islam" (Duval 1998: 67). Other women are now doing as she did. They are asserting their higher loyalty to an Islam that may contingently supersede kinship loyalties. Traditional institutions are changing under our eyes, and women are learning how to derive positive use from the symbols and rhetoric designed to contain them. Women who wish to retain control over their bodies and minds and to enter and remain in decision-making positions will have to develop a form of social, political, and religious criticism that I define in the next chapter as "multiple critique."

During the summer of 1995, I attended one of al-Ghazali's Monday morning sessions in her downtown Cairo apartment. I was ushered into her august presence by one of her young male disciples. Sitting behind her desk swathed in meters of cream-colored muslin, she ordered that I be given a copy of the first volume of her interpretation of the Qur'an. Entitled *Views on the Book of God*, it had come out the previous year. Later, I read parts of the book. Her interpretations were carefully conservative. This is not surprising, since her religious and social position did not allow her to conduct an Islamic feminist hermeneutics. After the preliminary formalities were over we proceeded to what felt more like a lecture or a monologue than a conversation. She would listen to my questions and then record her answers on an old-fashioned tape recorder. I had one question that I was eager to ask: Did she believe that once the jihad had been successful in establishing the Islamic state women should return to the home? She sat quietly for a while without, as was her wont, stretching her hand out automatically to turn the recorder back on.

Women, she finally pronounced, should continue doing what they had been doing up to that point, their eventual status should be decided by the authorities in the new Islamic state. What about assuming public office? I asked. Certainly, she quickly replied, they could work in the new government. Not president, of course. She smiled. Perhaps prime minister.

5

Multiple Critique

In 1995 the Algerian activist Khalida Messaoudi gave an interview to Elisabeth Schemla about her life since she was condemned to death by the Algerian Islamists the Front Islamique de Salut (FIS). She tells a story of the terrorization of intellectuals and particularly of women. Interspersed in the criticism is a surprising passage about women within the movement and how the FIS have empowered them:

The hidjab (or, veil) is one of the instruments of identification FIS has given women, but it isn't the only one. The FIS has also provided them with a mode of political speech the FLN (Front de Libération Nationale) never gave them . . . they speak, whereas before they had obstinately kept their mouths shut! Suddenly, they have a way of speaking, ideas *they* can defend and for which they are even willing to go out and demonstrate in the streets . . . the FIS gives them a place in which they can use this political speech, a place that tradition has always barred them from entering, a place outside. That is the mosque . . . women also acquire an identity there that is very difficult to contest, because it is endowed with an unparalleled power: the force of the sacred. (Messaoudi 1998: 113)

Messaoudi would seem to be an odd source to quote about the positive impact of Islamist ideology on the status of women. They did, after all, condemn her to death! But it is because of this very oddity that I find her testimony so powerful and persuasive. Even though she compares contemporary Islamists in Algeria favorably with the FLN, the nationalists who only pretended to give women rights, she is not defending them. Instead, she is showing how their system is backfiring. Women inside the movement are recognizing spaces of empowerment in an ideology intended to silence and marginalize them. Using the language and logic of their male counterparts, Islamist women are fashioning an identity that, as Messaoudi says, is very difficult to contest. After all, it is an identity forged within Islamism and therefore imbued with the force of the sacred. Messaoudi goes on to describe how "fundamentalist marriage" is free of traditional bonds since the couple is not obliged to consult the family, but only the "party of God." All they need "is the blessing of the instructor-imam" (114). They can claim their rights as part of a local community with transnational connections.

Feminists committed to their Islamic identity are creating a transnational sense of belonging, resistance, and steadfastness through their behavior but also through the hermeneutical and historical texts they are producing. I have come to believe that the effectiveness of an Islamic feminist discourse relies on the ability to recognize and exploit fissures in the system even while seeming to accede to its traditional norms and expectations. Despite their passive representations, some women are actively situating themselves as critics and reformers of transnational institutions that disadvantage or actually harm them. Like their male kin, compatriots, and coreligionists, they are struggling with the problems and challenges left behind by colonial rule. The European colonizers may have left Arab soil, but they have also left behind a burden of colonial legacies that link different Arab nations with a global system that may or may not include them in its purview. Women are peculiarly vulnerable where their men are most threatened. The men's disempowerment may force them to take extreme measures, and they may even commit violence against their women so as to recuperate a measure of status and dignity. Yet more often, Islamist men symbolically foreground women, but then relegate them to the political margins. Rejecting this passive characterization of their experiences, some are developing a multilayered Islamic feminist discourse that allows them to engage with and criticize individuals, institutions, and systems that limit and oppress them. At the same time, they maintain their Islamic bona fides so that they are not caught in their own rhetoric.

This oppositional stance I call *multiple critique*. It is a term I have coined from two others: Abdelkebir Khatibi uses the concept of *double critique*, the sociologist Deborah K. King *multiple consciousness*. In *Maghreb Pluriel* (1983) Khatibi describes the ways in which postcolonial subjects articulate an oppositional discourse that simultaneously targets local and global antagonists. In all of his writings, Khatibi focuses on duality and how it can be dialectically mobilized. By injecting gender criticism into his local/global critiques, we can imagine a third critique that moves beyond the dual. This third opens out onto a multiplicity of antagonists. It includes religious zealots and religious others, foreigners, homophobes, and women with different histories. Khatibi's approach allies with King's in her essay "Multiple Jeopardy, Multiple Consciousness: The Context of a Black Feminist Ideology." She describes the "multiple jeopardy" of black women who are "marginal to both the movements for women's liberation and black liberation irrespective of our victimization under the dual discrimination of racism and sexism" (King 1985: 299). This multiple jeopardy, however, creates the conditions for these women to have a multiple consciousness. This concept, derived from W. E. B. Du Bois's double consciousness, is a powerful tool for multiply centering and then affirming the self. King concludes with the assertion that black women who have been characterized as victims are now challenging the various systems that oppress and exclude them. She does not, however, describe how such an oppositional praxis might work.

Since black American women's experience of marginalization as they fall through the cracks of race and gender resembles that of postcolonial Arab Muslim women, I draw on the insights provided by King's notions of multiple jeopardy and multiple consciousness. Yet there is a major difference between the histories of black women in the United States and Muslim Arab women under colonial rule. Whereas women of African descent brought into the slave economy of North America were crucially important to its flourishing and have been remembered as such, Muslim Arab women were separated from spaces occupied by the colonizers and then discursively excluded except as outsiders to colonial history. African-American women were necessary parts of an economic chain, while Muslim Arab women were turned into symbols whose bodies were disappeared.

Indeed, Angela Davis describes African women as central to the entire plantation community. They were forced to navigate between the Scylla of white men's desires and the Charybdis of black men's frustrations. At the heart of both white and black households, a few women became the bridge between the two, a crucial conduit for information and sometimes resistance. Additionally, they provided "the *only* labor of the slave community that could not be directly and immediately claimed by the oppressor" (Davis 1985: 205). To survive, these few women became strong and independent, yet that is how all the women are remembered, regardless of what their actual experiences might have been. The upshot is that strong women alongside weak men are sometimes described negatively as matriarchs. The label has stuck and, according to Davis, many black women today do not dare to criticize their community lest they be labeled treacherous and their men walk out. However, some, like Beth Richie, urge women "to identify the 'traps' of loyalty. We must demand equality in our communities and in our relationship with black men" (Richie 1985: 403).

This is precisely what Arab Muslim women do when they situate themselves as Islamic feminists. For them, however, the task is less charged because of their very different historical experience. Far from being at the epicenter of their own communities, or that of the colonizers, Muslim women were on the margins, languishing in harems. Unlike slave owners in North America, Europeans in the Muslim Arab world found themselves obliged to respect the line that separated the private from the public. To be able to rule the men effectively they had to leave the women in their segregated spaces. The Europeans interacted with or, better, controlled the Muslim men outside their homes. Women's autobiographies and fiction as well as court records describe a place of privacy where the colonizer could not go.

There are no stories of European men raping Muslim Arab women. So extreme was the separation of Christian man from the Muslim woman that even the prostitutes were protected from infidel contamination. In his analysis of the poor non-Muslim sectors of eighteenth- and nineteenth-century Tunis, Abdelhamed Larguèche writes that the Muslim prostitute "was reserved for the Muslim man alone. . . . Because she had to be protected against the desires of Christians, she contributed as a woman toward the preservation of the community's honor even as she became the site of its threat" (1999: 289). As Lebanese critic Mai Ghossoub writes, "What better symbol of cultural identity than the privacy of women, refuge *par excellence* of traditional values that the old colonialism could not reach and the new capitalism must not touch? The rigidity of the status of women in the family in the Arab world has been an innermost asylum of Arabo-Muslim identity" (1987: 4). What is germane to my argument in the story about the segregated spaces is not their workings as a domain of male domination, but rather their impenetrability to all outsiders, including especially European Christian men.

This history that does not include Muslim Arab women as objects of colonialism calls into question the global narrative of the totality of European domination. Because they were not ruled directly by non-Muslim strangers, these women can imagine a pure, empty past they can fill with the kinds of experiences that allow them to be strong, oppositional but also loyal *today*. Marginal under colonialism, their history is not compromised. They can hold on to communal, national, and transnational religious ties without risking charges of treachery or complicity.

While the men were locked into a relationship with the colonizers that persists and continues to influence their choices and behaviors, women's spaces became the imagined heart of the authentic, ahistorical, uncontaminated Muslim nation. Women are more free to establish links and networks outside their primary affiliations even as they remain alert to others' needs and desires that they must negotiate and deflect. Those who choose to position themselves as Islamic feminists may find ways to go beyond multiple consciousness to multiple critique. When I use this term I am not in any way referring to some form of identity politics.

In identity politics, one's own identity or constellation of identities becomes the authorizing position from which to speak and to deauthorize the language of those not similarly placed. Identity politics pays little mind to others' perceptions, but rather focuses on the subject. Multiple critique, while it requires the same self-awareness, retains multiple consciousness of others. Multiple critique is not a fixed authorizing mechanism but a fluid discursive strategy taken up from multiple speaking positions. It allows for conversations with many interlocutors on many different topics. Unlike identity politics, which depends on an essentialized identity, multiple critique allows for identitarian contradictions that respond to others' silencing moves. The individual's goal is to remain in the community out of which she is speaking, even when she criticizes its problems. Multiple critique involves alliances and various forms of networking activities.

Critical Networking

In the mid-1980s and almost simultaneously, official networks concerned with the situation of Muslim women and women in Islamic societies began to form on an international scale. Muslim women who had been caught in webs of influences, which determine "for the individual woman what is probable, possible, or out of bounds" (Shaheed 1995: 78), turned to building their own webs, or networks. Sisters in Islam in Malaysia, the Federation of Muslim Women's Associations of Nigeria, Women Living Under Muslim Laws (WLUML) in France, the Association Indépendante pour le Triomphe des Droits des Femmes in Algeria as well as the various Salafi, Ikhwani, and Tablighi

Islamist movements in Asia and Africa began to connect women within and beyond their local associations.

In the 1990s women's nongovernmental associations (NGOs) have grown at an unprecedented pace. A few examples will serve as illustration. In 1996 a group of Yemeni scholars and lawyers came together to protest the proposed revision of the Personal Status Law. Meeting in each other's homes, they listened to invited religious scholars and strategized with women from within the Islamist Islah Party. Margot Badran writes, "Yemeni feminist activists are refusing to get caught up in a binary secular/religious framework. Activist women across the spectrum speak an Islamic language as they practice their feminism and a feminist language as they practice Islam" (1999: 164–68). In the mid-1990s a group of Maghrebian women formed Collectif 95 in order to oppose the imposition of a uniform family law in all Arab states. They "networked to preempt this by producing a counter-draft proposal for a uniform code of the family based on gender equality" (Shaheed 1995: 96–97).

Valentine Moghadam describes these kinds of NGOs as part of "a global trend in the expansion of civil society," as the state abdicates responsibilities it used to shoulder (1997: 49). I believe that the Internet and the introduction of the World Wide Web in the 1990s are expanding civil society even further to include women on an unprecedented scale. Islamic feminist groups are going online. For example, in 1992 English-speaking women married to Kuwaitis founded the Women's Association and Society for Islamic Learning and Awareness (WASILA). Their homepage describes their mission as the creation of "a base where they could study, practice and promote Islam, as well as socialize in an Islamic environment, and improve the community in whatever ways they could." In the United States, the Muslim Women's Help Network contributes to the establishment of a model Muslim society to help the needy. In Canada, the Federation of Muslim Women/La Federation des Femmes Musulmanes describes itself as "a group of active and dynamic women who are committed to the well-being of our community. We are dedicated to enhancing the quality of Muslim women's lives in Canada." And groups that were already formed, like Women Living Under Muslim Laws, went online as soon as possible.

These new information networks are empowering groups of women who had not before thought of themselves as members of any kind of community beyond that of kin or locale. Algerian Marie-Aimée Hélie-Lucas, founder in 1986 of WLUML, stated that her agenda was internationalism: "We must exchange information and support one another. We must create such solidarity so that we will be able to retain control over our protest. . . . Women and women's groups from seventeen countries or communities now communicate with each other through the Network, ask for documentation, compare so-called Muslim laws in different countries, send appeals for solidarity, inform each other about their strategies in very practical terms. . . . Internationalism must prevail over nationalism" (1990: 113–14). By emphasizing their religious identity, participants and subscribers to these real and virtual Islamic feminist networks are finding ways to resist identification of their goals as Western-inspired, and, above all, to gain respect and consideration for their demands.

The revolution in information technology is allowing Muslim women, some of whom may be physically confined to gendered spaces, to think of associations with others that will not compromise them morally. The situation of women in Saudi Arabia may be emblematic. In March 1999 the government allowed Internet service providers (ISPs) to work on Saudi soil, and by the end of the year over 100,000 people had subscribed. In Riyadh I met with Nawaf al-Fawzan, the managing director of Awalnet, the leading Saudi ISP, which has a women's office and computer center. He told me that Awalnet was designed with women in mind, since they are the economic decision makers in Saudi households.

An article in the November 7, 1999, *Saudi Gazette* reported that women are the ones spending the most time at their computer terminals, and the trend is increasing. It is too early to know what the cultural outcome will be, but the fact that this radically new form of connection among the most disconnected section of the population has caught on so widely is suggestive. Sex segregation seems to have enhanced networking among women, particularly those between the ages of twenty and thirty-five. This is the cohort out of which a new generation of potential leaders may be drawn. In a sex-segregated society, men and women must form parallel communities, *both of which must function in the public sphere.* Saudi women, more than others, must be educated and trained to do what the men do. They must be bankers, teachers, professors, and university administrators at all levels, doctors, surgeons, and journalists. They must be able to interact with each other and if necessary with outsiders. Information technology enhances these interactions: telephones, closed-circuit television as well as satellite television beaming in potentially forbidden information, and now the Internet. Today, Saudi women can connect through networks like Awalnet's Laki Anti or the France-based WLUML and learn more about their rights.

Information is running rampant. Governments are losing control of transnational broadcasting by satellite television stations. People now have uncensored access to stations like the radical Qatari Jazira that broadcasts interviews with controversial personalities. For example on May 5, 1998, the "Opposite Direction" of Jazia featured Nawal El Saadawi in conversation with an Islamist shaykh. He was Yusuf al-Badri, the shaykh responsible for starting the campaign against the Egyptian scholar Nasr Hamid Abu Zayd. He had been instrumental in taking Abu Zayd to Sharia court and having him declared an apostate because of his liberal interpretations of the Qur'an. In Egypt, al-Badri was able to go so far as to demand that the wife of the recently declared "apostate" divorce her husband.

However, in Qatar when confronted by El Saadawi, he was not so successful. The live show was a fiasco for him. Several Saudis who saw the show told me that this was a setup. Why? Because the Jazira people had deliberately chosen a "stupid shaykh" whom El Saadawi had infuriated and left speechless. El Saadawi's version of the event, however, is quite different! In a conversation in December 1999 she complained to me that in fact she had not had a chance to say anything: "Every time I opened my mouth to say something, he would start screaming. I had many things to say but he would not let me speak. When I went to Lebanon, people said to me, Shame on you, Nawal, you destroyed him! And I had to reply, No, I did not! He destroyed himself!"

Whatever the reality of the story, the perception for all was the same. Arabs all over the Middle East and North Africa witnessed a feminist get the better of an Islamist on his own scriptural territory. For some, this was a bad thing and a sign that El Saadawi was opposed to Islam, the more dangerously so because they described her as having been able to muster sources and quotations with such ease. For others, this was a triumph of a Muslim woman's intelligence, and they took pride in her achievement, if only sotto voce! While I was in Saudi Arabia, there was a virtual ban on even mentioning Nawal's name. I doubt that the ban will last, but rather that it may become yet another banner under which to demand a woman's right to seek knowledge and to interpret religious texts in a way that is more friendly to women.

Why focus on Saudi Arabia and its women? First of all, Saudi Arabia is the emblematic Muslim nation. It is the direction of prayer for observant Muslims five times a day. It is a polity that has organized itself around Islam and has taken responsibility for the guardianship of Islam's two most holy sites, Mecca and Medina. It is a legal and political system that derives directly from scripture. It is a radically sex-segregated society that insists on the importance of appearance. It is already tribalized in a world that Manuel Castells has described as moving ever more in the direction of general tribalization as communes of resistance and localized identities are mobilizing to hold on to diversity as empowering but also as generating globalized value. It is also a country that is increasingly networking with the rest of the world and which is now anticipating and preparing for revolutionary change.

Within this system women are cast as symbolically important. They are the physical markers of social norms. The more visible their otherness, the more they must remain within the moral boundaries. One key element has been the physical absence of women from public space occupied by men. Yet the change is already there just below the surface. It is not insignificant that Fatima Naseef is telling women everywhere that one of their major rights is the right to seek knowledge. In a country where the ruler appoints religious authorities whose task is to interpret the scriptures, injunctions to women to learn their rights so that they know how to interpret the scriptures for themselves might be construed as subversive. Where the state appoints and controls who interprets religious texts and consequently commands individual spiritual loyalty, women are learning that in Islam no one has the right to interpose himself between the reader of scripture and the text. Dr. Fatima and Samira Jamjum are talking weekly to huge crowds of women and telling them what their religious, social, economic, and political rights are. When I asked Dr. Fatima who her disciples were she replied, "Every woman who comes to listen to me is becoming a teacher of one or two more women." She knows what she is doing. She is encouraging women to learn their God-given rights and to take responsibility for making society, men, and the government accountable for their claim to be the model Muslims.

As access to cyberspace in the Arab world opens up, some are beginning to speculate on the cultural implications of the technology revolution. How is information turned into knowledge, and knowledge transformed into action? How does individual empowerment through knowledge become a communal agenda? Some argue that even within these virtual communities women have to deal with continued pressures exerted by patriarchal systems (Wheeler 1998). Castells, on the other hand, foresees "uncontrollable connectedness" that entails individuals tranforming themselves, "significantly mixing spirituality, advanced technology (chemicals, biology and laser), global business connections, and the culture of millenarist doom" (1996: 23–24). From within this web of connections, cyberspace may offer liberatory prospects.

Anthropologist Arturo Escobar extends this utopian scenario to imagine that networks will produce new political actors and "cybercultures that resist, transform or present alternatives to the dominant virtual and real worlds . . . from the corridors of cyberspace can thus be launched a defence of place and place-based ecological and cultural practices which might, in turn, transform the worlds that the dominant networks help to create" (1995: 32–33). Escobar describes women, environmentalists, and "movements in the Third World" as being most likely to succeed in these kinds of oppositional practices because of their historical attachment to *places*. Optimistically, he concludes that "new modes of knowing, being and doing based on the principles of interactivity, positionality and connectivity are emerging from the engagement of place-based political actors with new technologies" (33). As the reach of the Internet grows, it will be hard for anyone to escape its influence.

In the 1990s, networking across the globe with friends and strangers started to become commonplace. Previous understandings of identity and communal belonging were being questioned. Intimate relationships, as in the family or between men and women, were the most transformed, so that "social movements and cultural projects built around identities in the Information Age . . . do not originate within the institutions of civil society. They introduce, from the outset, an alternative logic." This logic forms the foundation for what Castells calls "communes of resistance identity" (1997: 346–48, 351) within network states.

Women from within conservative religious associations are creating communes of resistance identity that articulate such an alternative logic. Andrea Rugh has observed Egyptian Islamist movements in which "individuals operate more independently from their families than has been the custom in the past. . . . In steering individuals toward loyalty to the *umma*, or community of Muslim believers, fundamentalist ideology gives direction to this tendency, and ultimately encourages a reorganization of society integrated at the suprafamilial level" (1993: 151). Individuals are weighing family and *umma* loyalties, reconsidering who is responsible for what. There is a quiet consensus that "women's roles are now different—that women take a more active, even though still secondary, role in formal religious and public life" (175–77). This transformation in notions of obedience, belonging, and activism has already been seen in connection with al-Ghazali's prison memoirs, where the needs of jihad changed gender norms, and the Islamic state displaced the family as the primary unit of belonging. Loyalty to God supersedes all else.

These changes may be temporary, a contingent response to globalization by individuals in specific kinds of settings. But what is remarkable is that this phenomenon is appearing throughout the Arab world and beyond. It mimics what was happening in the seventh century when Muhammad brought his socialist and feminist revolution to the feuding, patriarchal tribes of Arabia. Divisive tribal loyalties gave way to submission to God through participation in the new religious community. In the same way, today's atomizing family and national loyalties are taking second place to *da'wa*, whose goal is the founding of the transnational Islamic state uniting Muslims all over the world.

This transfer of primary allegiance from biological father to Divine Father allows individuals to reconsider their notions of hierarchy as well as their relationships with those in positions of authority. Blind obedience gives way to "individual conscience— shaped by the values and norms of the movement" (176). A socioreligious movement whose aim is to bring the community back to traditional norms has ironically opened up possibilities for women's independence and individual action within alternative communities that would otherwise be inconceivable.

Women, whether or not they be Islamists like al-Ghazali or the women whom Messaoudi and Rugh describe, have new opportunities. Some are learning how to make the system work for them. The ones who project an Islamic feminist identity are using this new community-centered logic to empower themselves and to prevent their bodies from continuing to be the site of struggle for control of public space. They are assuming responsibility for naming themselves and assigning their own meanings to their appearance and actions. Wary of political separatism, they are joining forces with others so as not to remain isolated and, therefore, unable to act. This is what Women Against Fundamentalism (WAF) are doing in Britain today. Mobilized by the Salman Rushdie affair in 1989, which heightened the sense of communalism in Britain, a group of South Asian, Jewish, Irish, and Iranian women came together as WAF. Despite utterly different histories, they shared an agenda to resist local extremist groups (Connolly and Patel 1997: 386). What matters when forming such strategic alliances is that individuals balance their religious loyalties with national, local, class, ethnic, or any other critical allegiances.

Cyber networking allows women to forestall expansion of male power and to make their own decisions about what others claim are universal imperatives. Sifting through the mass of information newly available to them, they can test local laws against their own understandings of Sharia. Unlike official organizations that bring bodies together and therefore expose individuals in segregated societies to restrictions and reprisals, cybernetworks construct virtual links that connect isolated individuals in a process of vital information exchange "without trying either to homogenize the diversity of people or to control their autonomy in matters of political or personal choice. . . . They also provide an alternative reference point for women . . . and legitimacy for change" (Shaheed 1995: 97). In cybernetworks, women can hold on to the specificity of their identities and local issues while linking with others. A critical mass of networks may "transform women's struggles for survival into workable strategies for bringing about a gender-equitable society, whether in the Muslim world or elsewhere" (98), but only as long as political and personal struggles continue simultaneously.

Coalition building and networking are as risky as they are necessary. In situations where male religious authorities are trying to control women and deprive them of Islamically sanctioned rights, it may be necessary for women to adopt an Islamic feminist agenda that will need outside support. In the process they risk allying themselves with people who would like to benefit from the fact that Muslims are divided among themselves. Unexpected antagonists are other women, and those of their compatriots who are secular, but above all white Western feminists. The challenge is how to collaborate "without losing the specificity of the concrete struggles of different women" (Connolly and Patel 1997: 381). They are suspicious of appeals to "international feminism" because such a global movement may be implicated in anti-Islamic imperialist ideologies and practices. This was why Zaynab al-Ghazali rejected Huda Shaarawi's Egyptian Feminist Union and established her own Muslim Ladies' Association. Yet they may at the very same moment, and again like al-Ghazali, consider Western or westernized feminists as possible partners in contingent, single-issue coalitions once they have eschewed such complicities. In a context shaped by colonial legacies, women retaining the memory of colonial practices of racialization and subjugation—even if they were not direct targets—may doubt the possibilities of finding a project in which all feel they share a stake. Even if they agree on antipatriarchal goals, how can Algerian women confronting fundamentalism at home trust the French granddaughters of their previous colonizers who insist that they demand their rights and confront their fathers, husbands, brothers, and sons? How can Egyptian and Sudanese women struggling with the problem of female genital mutilation trust American women who demand its abolition, even if they be of African heritage?

Full trust may never be possible, yet the need for alliances with different groups is often necessary. What is key is to know how and when to compromise. When Islam and resistance to neocolonialism are strong, Islamic feminists will be in a good position to link with outsiders and to critique the ways in which this opposition to globalization is being underwritten by the mobilization of women's bodies. When the religious identity of the group is under attack, the women can join with their men as Islamic feminists to assert an oppositional religiocultural identity. Their multiple consciousness gives them a position of strength from which to consider the possibilities of alliances others might reject. Some scholars, like Constance Buchanan and Afsaneh Najmabadi, argue that religion gives the tools to construct alliances that secular women may not trust because they consider religion to be a barrier to women's advancement. As mentioned above, this was the case for al-Ghazali during the struggle for Egyptian independence in 1952. It remains true in Pakistan today, where Islamists and secular women joined forces under the rubric of Women Against Rape, or WAR, "to organize jointly on issues of violence against women" (Rouse 1999: 207).

Assia Djebar, Fatima Mernissi, and Nawal El Saadawi reject Islamism, calling it the religion of a small, if vocal, minority who adopt a politics of violence because they have seen no other way of flourishing in the modern world and of saying no to Western hegemony. The religion that they invoke is the internationally significant political player, but it is also the individual faith system that rejects violence as it manages both internal and external conflict. It is only from within this global political and religious system that new visions of Islam in the world can be invented.

It is in withstanding the dictates of systems unfriendly to women, but remaining in these same communities, that Islamic feminists demonstrate most vividly how multiple critique works. They have recognized the importance of networking at all levels, but also the risks that such alliances present because to be with one group may entail apparent and involuntary opposition to others. This was what happened to an Arab friend of mine when the Taliban, an Islamist group in Afghanistan, came to power on September 27, 1996. To maintain confidentiality I shall call my friend Fatima al-Kindi and her recently veiled colleague Zaynab Sabah. Soon after Zaynab put on the ritual scarf, they had quarreled. Was the veil empowering or oppressive? As two middle-class female professors, they were assured a measure of each other's recognition and respect, and they argued the merits and dangers of women dressing in a way distinctive to a religion. Fatima accused Zaynab of false consciousness. Zaynab retorted that Fatima had not understood her. She was sanguine that the veil could not be used against her since it was she who had freely chosen to assume it.

Enter Ahmed, Zaynab's younger brother. He wanted to accompany his sister home. Zaynab was shocked. Who had given him this crazy idea? People, he retorted, had been whispering foul things about this woman who lived alone. She should cover her face and glove her hands.

"Ridiculous!" the two women exclaimed together.

They quizzed him about Islamic prescriptions concerning women's dress, correcting his misapprehension that the Qur'an mandates veiling. Zaynab repeated that it had been her choice to veil.

"I might take it off tomorrow!"

And with that, Ahmed stormed off.

They turned on the radio. Kabul: the Taliban have come to power. One of their first acts is to curtail women's rights: women must be totally covered and can no longer work in government offices. They will be recompensed for the salary. Girls' schools are to be closed. Fatima and Zaynab were stunned. Something had to be done to stop these madmen. They convened a student-faculty meeting to consider action, including coalitions with others, even non-Muslims since this was such a broad issue of gender discrimination. At the mention of the possibility of forming alliances with American and European women, the atmosphere became troubled. Fatima found herself lining up with Zaynab, who had objected to the closing of the girls' schools and the ban on women's employment in Afghanistan but had refused to condemn the veiling. What had happened? The images of the Muslim Woman and the Western Woman had intervened. Fatima and Zaynab had American and European women friends, but who else might join the mass appeal? They realized that they had to remain alert to the ways in which uninformed others might use Muslim women's attacks on the veil. They were prepared to change tactics even if such a change might involve apparently contradictory consciousness that moves from the highly individualized to the tightly collective as images are controlled and imposed.

Imageness

How can preconception built on the weak but resilient foundations of myth and image be overcome? Images are flat impressions that provide pieces of information. Like photographs, they frame and freeze a fragment of the real and then project it as the whole. What was dynamic and changing becomes static. Just as a snapshot provides a true, if partial, picture, so these cultural images contain some truth. That is why they are so hard to change.

Women are easily turned by outsiders into images that then become emblems of their culture, for within the culture itself women serve that same function. No matter how many chaste, modest American women an Asian Muslim may meet, no matter how many assertive, independent, unveiled Asian Muslim women an American may meet, the basic image may not change as these individuals are seen as exceptions to a rule that they thereby serve to reinforce. During the late 1980s I took a group of students to Morocco for a summer program. After we had been in Marrakesh for a few days, I asked them what they thought about the women. One student blurted out, "They are veiled." Others nodded in acquiescence. Astonished, I took them out into the street and asked them to look again as women sauntered past in all varieties of clothes. One or two were veiled. As usual. These images are the context of a first encounter between two people who know little if anything about each other. They may not change if they are not directly confronted and deconstructed.

The exchange in images of women between Arab and Western countries has been intense during the twentieth century and it has served as a barometer of cross-cultural attitudes. Although Arab women's journals from the 1890s until the outbreak of World War II were in general positively inclined toward strong Western role models, by the 1960s things had changed. Representations of American women became polarized between two evils: the Superwoman who sacrifices her family for her career, and the promiscuous symbol of the moral decadence into which the United States had plunged.

Conversely, Arab women's images were first filtered through Orientalist lenses—mysterious, alluring, secluded. As American contacts with the Arab world grew, the half-naked odalisque was replaced by the completely covered chattel who represented the oppressiveness of Arab patriarchy. The horrors of woman-hating Muslim societies, standard fare in the U.S. media, came to a head in the fall of 1990. As international forces were gathering in Kuwait and Saudi Arabia to attack Iraq, pundits of the U.S. media surmised the salutary impact that the presence of female American military personnel would have on Saudi society. On August 25, 1990, the *New York Times* published such an article, illustrated with two contrasting images: the Marine woman with her full pack next to a completely veiled woman. When in November some fifty Saudi women drove their cars across the Saudi capital of Riyadh, the media crowed in satisfaction: "Told you so!" It was as though it was the American women in the military who had inspired the insurrection.

The "truth" of the driving incident was quite otherwise. This demonstration put back a movement that was well on its way to success. Saudi women had for several years been winning their battle against the prohibition on women's driving. Their argument had been that only the wealthy could afford to hire full-time drivers and that being alone in a car with a strange man was more compromising than driving ever could be. The driving demonstration was not radical within the context of their struggle, but it became intolerable in view of the presence of these foreign troops. As long as non-Muslim, primarily Western, troops were on Saudi soil, women stood for the Saudi, Muslim difference. Whether that difference was morally superior or not depended on whether the speaker was Saudi or American. When these fifty or so women ceased to accept their roles as symbols but acted as individuals, they could no longer be contained unless they were punished. This punishment served the Saudi regime, whose projected self-image was thus safeguarded. Paradoxically, it served the U.S. government too, because it reinforced the image of a Saudi patriarchy so entrenched that even this powerful cultural intervention by American women could not finally work its wonders.

The image of Muslim women homogeneously oppressed by patriarchy has interfered in cross-cultural dialogue and understanding and, therefore, also in conducting multiple critique. Its role in communication needs to be understood. Communication, according to Roman Jakobson, is about the degree to which a message can pass between addresser and addressee "enabling both of them to enter and stay in conversation" (1990: 66). There is a language to be agreed upon and an appropriate context to be created so that the message may become "verbal or capable of being verbalized." A key factor, Jakobson asserts, is the "so-called emotive or 'expressive' function, focused on the addresser." This emotive function informs the context, which will change in accordance with the degree to which addresser and addressee feel that they are being accorded respect.

I propose that this model of communication must also include what I call "imageness," a visual reality that shapes consciousness. Unlike Jakobson's model of communication, images are rarely dynamic. The cultural photographs that we bring to a first encounter are unlikely to change; they fade in and out as they are needed. To draw attention to imageness is to acknowledge that interlocutors do not ever deal with the individual alone, or even with the individual contextualized, but have to contend with, and ideally overcome, the images they have of each other.

The image, which is always moving in and out of focus, marks, according to Homi Bhabha, "the site of an ambivalence. Its representation is always spatially split—it makes *present* something that is *absent*—and temporally deferred: it is the representation of a time that is always elsewhere, a repetition. The image is only ever an *appurtenance* to authority and identity; it must never be read mimetically as the appearance of a reality" (1994: 51). Certainly, the image is an appurtenance to authority, but not always as its assertion, rather as an attempt to seize power or to recover it. I question Bhabha's characterization of the image as a tool of power by those in power, as a top-down process. I contend that what he refers to as the "fixity in the ideological construction of otherness" is inherent in dialogue. It is not merely a function of colonial discourse (66). In other words, to name and mark otherness is not the exclusive privilege of power; rather, it is part of the contestation over power.

We name each other to gain control, if not over the other then over the situation. The fact that the slave cannot openly name the master does not mean that he does not do so. As James C. Scott has written, slaves have their hidden transcripts. When away from the surveilling look of the master they name him, waiting for the day when they can do so publicly. What is different in the postcolonial period is that hierarchical positions are constantly shifting (Scott 1990). It is no longer so clear from whom the transcript must be kept hidden. The basic dynamic, however, remains the same. This juggling of person and image persists throughout the life of a relationship. It is present not only during the acquainting period, but also during the continual struggle to negotiate the context of the message exchange. At the macrolevel, changing world politics and the consequent adjustments in media stereotyping of others will enhance or diminish the space the image takes up in calculations about whether contact is advisable or even possible. At the microlevel, changing personal relationships will dictate whether the image shrinks or grows. The image is a stereotype, not an archetype. It is not the same for all people but differs according to the situations of the addresser and the addressee. However, like an archetype, it lurks in the shadows.

Communication demands interaction and trust as each person covered by the image acknowledges and welcomes a similar personal stake in learning to know the other and thereby revealing and sometimes transforming the self. The process is dynamic also, so that it may take unexpected turns, even reverse itself. The layers of complexity so carefully accumulated may be stripped away if the context changes. This is the case because the construction and deconstruction of images is such a volatile, precarious process serving several purposes. Should the image return, it will do so reinforced by the knowledge of what it conceals. This return brings disappointment, anger, and often a sense of betrayal: "You are, after all, what they said you are."

The Weight of the Veil

Images we have of each other are part of the baggage we bring to dialogue. Sometimes we are at the mercy of our image; sometimes we hide behind it; sometimes we act *as though* neither of us had an image of the other. Sometimes, those ideal times, the image disappears and the contact is unmediated by the myth. Then we can act as individuals between whom messages pass easily. It is the degree to which the image is present in dialogue that affects the ways in which identity is articulated. The less clear and present the image, the less community-centered and the more individuated will be the sense of self projected. The more the image interposes itself between the addresser and the addressee, the more community-defined will be the individual identity. This is particularly the case for Muslim women when they veil.

The image of Muslim women as passive and oppressed has gained currency because it signifies beyond itself to a general category, such as a faith and a culture. In both cases their look is the same: they are more or less exotic, more or less veiled, more or less available, more or less oppressed. This is the image with which they will always have to contend.

The image of the veiled woman, as Homi Bhabha writes about images in general, "gives access to an 'identity' which is predicated as much on mastery and pleasure as it is on anxiety and defence, for it is a form of multiple and contradictory belief in its recognition of difference and disavowal of it" (1994: 75). How can preconception accommodate lived reality? How can individuals control what they wish to project and what is projected onto them? Despite geographic, linguistic, racial, ethnic, religious, and cultural diversity among Muslim women, what counts from the outside is their shared faith. After all, we can more easily identify as Muslim, rather than Egyptian or Pakistani, a woman we see in some form of purdah. The Muslim Woman image overrides all others to constitute these women's primary identity.

Muslim women's physical appearance becomes a crucial element in the observer's interpretation of whether the cohesiveness of the international Islamic community is a good or a bad thing. During the *hajj*, gender differences seem to disappear: we see men and women together circumambulating the Kaaba, all dressed in the same simple white cloth. That women in what are assumed to be highly segregated societies dress exactly the same as the men and participate equally with them in all the rituals shows how democratic Islam can be. This benign monolithic image, however, is more often assigned malevolent meaning. *The Fundamental Question*, a film made for classroom use, talks about Islamic fundamentalism as though it were Islam. This internationally connected movement is the new enemy in the post–cold war era. In contrast with the *hajj* image, this one *highlights gender differences*. This is an anti-West men's movement that universally excludes women. Images of covered women epitomize Islam. These women's bodies serve as icons of Muslim otherness. When among themselves and performing the most sacred duty of their religion, they are so united that no difference, not even that of gender, can undermine their seamless oneness. When confronting outsiders, they remain united as a people, split as to gender.

Such images fit into and exacerbate our preconceptions. All of these women represent something other than themselves. On the one hand, the domestic prisoners stand for the local patriarchy with its accoutrements of privilege dependent on the control of women; they are the empty vessels through which pass notions of honor and shame. On the other hand, fierce and face-less, these women confront us with the total mobilization of a nation on behalf of its beliefs. If religiously conservative men allow their women to participate in politics and even to bear guns and to fight, their commitment to their cause must be total.

The veil symbolizes belonging to a religious community that is both patriarchal and powerful, but beyond it has many mean-ings. While some of these meanings are negative, others are empowering. Assessment of the veil's value may depend on where the women live. If their society is one in which the norm is for women to veil, they will become invisible once they veil. However, in a multicultural context where many religious obser-vances are tolerated, the veiled woman will stand out. The United Arab Emirates woman shopping in the Marble Arch Marks & Spencer in London is such an example; she shocks by the stark contrast between her all-enveloping black cloth and mask, or *batul,* and her husband's blue jeans and T-shirt. Another example of such exceptionality can be found among African-American women who joined the Nation of Islam in the 1960s. Far from being disempowered by the veil, or what they called the *khimar* and sometimes the "uniform," they used it to symbol-ize their freedom and social worth in a community that valued its women and rejected their previous sexual objectification under slavery.

Even when women make their own decisions concerning the veil, their decision may be used by others to serve other goals. In the 1990s, the new veil that some Jordanian and Algerian women chose has been used to represent their "transnational anti-Western sentiments in its international uniformity. The image of the young veiled woman behind the computer is part of national pride" (Jansen 1998: 90). The individual, perhaps oppositional, choice has been symbolically co-opted for nationalist purposes. Veiled women highlight the sexually conservative character of the modern community in which they live and function. Muslim women's public prominence is not only symbolic; it is also actual. The more Muslim women are policed, the more visible they become. It matters less whether they have chosen the veil or were forced to do so. Unlike the traditional covering, the new veil marks a woman as religiously observant, and as someone whose honor men are obliged to safeguard.

The veil can also be actively used to voice protests and perhaps to ameliorate conditions in at least "three dimensions of inequality: in relations of gender, class, and global position" (Duval 1998: 64). In her study of the lives of lower middle class women in Cairo who have been veiling since the 1970s, Arlene Macleod opens up a new way to understand the contradictions involved in the assumption of the veil in a modernizing society. Without in any way minimizing the religious importance of the decision to veil, she points out the socioeconomic constraints that come into play in this decision. She explains that these Cairene women must have an income if they and their families wish to retain their precarious lower-middle-class status. In the growing conservatism of their environment, working women must beware of the accusation of moral looseness when away from their homes. Wearing the veil assures everyone that these women will not be harassed in the streets and in the workplace, but also that they have become honorable women (Macleod 1991).

Nawal El Saadawi absolutely rejects any notion of the veil's utility for women. How can this emblem of sexuality and men's desire possibly serve women? For El Saadawi, the woman who wears a veil is drawing attention to her body as much as the woman who wanders the streets naked. The covered woman is so obsessed by the dangers of her body that she can think of nothing else and she might as well have veiled her mind. El Saadawi's slogan, which became the mission of the Arab Women's Solidarity Association that El Saadawi founded in 1982, is "Removing the Veil from the Mind." Like other Islamic feminists, El Saadawi has used the Qur'an and Traditions to bolster her claim that the veil is not Islamic. Echoing the sentiments of Nazira Zayn al-Din (Zayn al-Din 1998: 113–20), she adds that the veil is a primitive symbol of slavery, evidence of the men's commodification of the women they "own."

Those who reject the possibility that Nawal El Saadawi is an Islamic feminist do not understand why or how she threatens the religious establishment. In 1993, Yasir Farahat published *The Confrontation: Nawal El Saadawi in the Witness Stand.* It contains the proceedings of a mock trial by eight religious judges, three men and five women, who debate the premises underlying her rejection of the veil and polygyny as un-Islamic. Unable to refute her point about the veil's role in accentuating rather than concealing the woman's body, Imam [*sic*] Shaykh al-Sha'rawi goes so far as to prove her point for her. The reason that women must veil is not Qur'anic but rather because of men's, especially old men's, lechery. What can you expect if a man accustomed to the unsightly wrinkles of his forty- or fifty-year-old wife walks out into the streets where luscious maidens parade their bodies? He will be tormented and "when he returns home he will begin to compare," and there may come a point when the woman is so old and ugly that "no one will want to approach her to speak with her" (Farahat 1993: 182–83)! Perhaps including God? When El Saadawi writes in her novel *Innocence of the Devil* that God refuses to talk with women, she is not fabulating, for women have been told that during menstruation they should not touch the Qur'an nor should they pray and fast. For these judges, the only way to prevent trouble is for all women to be covered.

One of Farahat's five judges is Zaynab al-Ghazali. She supports Shaykh al-Sha'rawi and dismisses El Saadawi as "stupid" (178). The other women judges, however, are less crude. Dr. Amina Nusayr, dean of the girls' college in al-Azhar, and Dr. Maryam al-Daghistani, a professor in the same college, both address El Saadawi respectfully as "a Muslim who believes in the angels, the prophets and what was revealed in the Qur'an" (191, 196). Yet they go on to underscore Shaykh al-Sha'rawi's obsession with the *fitna* (a word meaning both "attractiveness" and "sedition") of women's bodies before they age. To cover this temptation, this femininity, is the only way for women to be able to function with men. El Saadawi's claim that to cover the body is to draw attention to it and thus to cover the mind is unanswerable. No arguments about the veil not covering face and hands can disprove that the veil is the body is the mind. The major difference between El Saadawi and her judges is that they believe that women are bodies *before* putting on the veil, whereas the accused claims that it is *after* veiling that women become bodies. Despite the weakness of these authorities' rejoinders to El Saadawi's impassioned criticism of what she argues are un-Islamic norms imposed on women so as to subjugate them, she was considered by some to be heretical. Her placement on the death list of some extremist Islamist groups led to a four-year exile spent primarily at Duke University in North Carolina.

Leila Ahmed provides an intermediate position on veiled women and their feminist attitudes. Quoting from a survey with veiled and unveiled women that Zeinab Radwan conducted in 1982, she comments on the remarkable similarities between both groups on issues of human rights and especially the inherent justice of Islam. Some unveiled women even endorsed the imposition of Islamic law (1992: 227–28). Their condition was that it not be codified according to the norms of what Ahmed calls "establishment Islam," which is unambiguous in the way it perceives and hierarchizes gender relations. It eliminates "those who challenge its authority or its particular understanding of Islam, including other Muslims intent on heeding the ethical over the doctrinal voice" (230). Ahmed separates the veiling issue from establishment Islam so as to allow for women's agency and the possibility of making real choices.

The image of the veil today is riddled with contradictions. It imprisons and liberates. Whether the veil is imposed or chosen, however, it is an item of clothing that each woman daily engages, aware of the symbolic baggage it carries. As she looks at her reflection in the morning to hide her hair and adjust the cloth, this veiled woman daily reaffirms the fact that her body marks her out morally and sexually—in other words, as a religious and as a female person. Daily this veiled woman has a multiple consciousness of herself, as she sees herself, as her community sees her, and as outsider men and women see her. She must continually negotiate the symbolism of this piece of cloth that is so saturated with patriarchal meaning that it is difficult to appropriate for feminist purposes. She must constantly remember how the veil functions in constructing her image.

Conclusion

The speaking position adopted by Islamic feminists is dictated by context and the degree to which this context gives them a sense of worth and dignity that elicits respect and, therefore, frees them from the fear of the return of the image. At the local level, authoritarian governments, poverty, and resurgent religious expression invite more gender-specific responses. At the global level, nationalisms, neocolonialism, and mass migration, especially postcolonial immigrant community building, demand another way of speaking. This rhetoric may involve the expedient use of homogenizing generalizations that allow the injured individual to claim allegiance to a group that thus shares the injury and becomes collectively responsible for its repair. This individual may then charge the same group for causing another injury. When Islamic feminists do not feel under siege as women, they can denounce local patriarchal assumptions; when they do not feel threatened as Muslims, they can challenge Islamic prescriptions unfavorable to women. As the Iranian sociologist Ziba Mir-Husseini writes, "a feminist re-reading of the *shari'a* is possible—even becomes inevitable—when Islam is no longer part of the oppositional discourse in national politics. This is so because once the custodians of the *shari'a* are in power, they have to deal with the contradictory aims set by their own agenda" (1996: 286). In other words, when Islam is no longer part of the oppositional discourse, women can claim their Islamic rights. If the family is said to be the most important unit in society and women are said to occupy the most important place in the family, then the many laws affecting them adversely should be revised.

The key to understanding Islamic feminist discursive strategies is to take cognizance of our own. We must examine both the images and the image makers. We need to understand how images naturalize cultural, political, geographical, and religious differences. I have to be sensitive to the moment when I cease to be the individual miriam cooke and come to be seen as part of a group of U.S. neo-imperialist, feminist scholars. Conversely, I must remain alert to the corollary changes happening to my interlocutor. To pay multiple attention to the slide across the spectrum bridging communal and individual identity projection is a skill that is integral to the practice of multiple critique. It is a skill that must be learned if dialogue is to be possible.

To speak of oneself as part of a community in which one has a particular position is not to be mired in the past, it is to find oneself in need of such a broad and overarching identification. To invoke binaries of individual and community orientation for particular groups of people is to construct a discourse of power based on a false dichotomization: *They* are not like *us* so we cannot deal with them. Islamic feminist discourse, however, reveals that the individual and the community are always in tension with each other. Laws that target the one without the other serve the interests of those in power. In the absence of any divinely sanctioned authority, the shape of the religion and the interpretation of its laws become a matter for everyone to engage simultaneously at the individual and communal levels.

When Muslims emphasize the importance of community, they may have made an expedient decision based on a perception that they have been denied recognition because of who they are as national, racial, ethnic, sexed individuals. At that point, they will demand respect for that aspect of their identity that has incurred the misrecognition. This single allegiance is thus contingent. Back in safe space, they are once again at ease with their multiple, multicultural, multifaceted selves.

This ceaseless move between individuated and communalized identities is a function of misrecognition: *where* we are and *with whom* changes *how* we speak; it may even change *what* we say. Once we understand how our behavior and speech are constantly changing, how untrue we usually are to any sense of a stable self, we can recognize a similar process in others without automatically characterizing them as radically other. We can begin to make sense of contradictions in identity performances rather than smugly pointing to them as inconsistencies at best or deceitfulness at worst. To recognize in others' behavior our own is the first step toward moderating the images that crush individuality and make it so hard to see the commonalities that are the basis for mutual understanding and respect. Images are part of who we are and of the ways in which we interact with others, however close or familiar they may seem. If we cannot—and I suspect we cannot—overcome the interference of the image, we must learn to listen to the image speak.

6

Changing the Subject

During the past twenty years, Arab Muslim women have become an increasingly popular topic of study in the United States. Courses on women and Islam are becoming part of the regular offerings of departments of religious studies, history, politics, and women's studies. A new contingent of scholars and students is examining the connections among gender, women, and religion in Muslim contexts. Some scholars who had studied the Arab world from a gender-blind perspective began to recognize how their work undergirded a masculinist approach to a society already stigmatized as reactionary and patriarchal. Others trained at the height of second-wave feminism turned away from their teachers' focus on the public space that was occupied by men to examine that other public space, the part occupied by women. Although most of the early research was done by U.S. and European women, by the mid-1980s a new generation of scholars of Arab Muslim women appeared. They were Arab-American women who, as a result of the impact of political events in the Middle East and North Africa on U.S. policy and public opinion, recognized how scholarship on Arab Muslim women was influencing the U.S. imaginary of the Arab world.

To understand these scholars' perspectives and self-positioning we need to cast a quick look over the history of Arab migration to the United States during the twentieth century. This history helps to explain the growing involvement of Arab-Americans in the production of knowledge about the Arab world, and particularly its most sensitive aspect, Muslim women.

A key component of this history is race as marked by color. Nowhere in the Arab world does color of skin matter as much as it does in the United States, where percentages of color are carefully computed so as to calculate degrees of benefit. For Americans who fall outside clear categories defined by continent of origin, which is generally equated with skin color, U.S. identity may become a problem. El Saadawi tells of her alarm when she came to the U.S. South in the early 1960s. Upon entering the women's room of a public university, she read two signs above two doors: "White" and "Black." She was forced to choose between these doors. Looking at her arms, she could not decide which color was closest to hers. So, understanding the meaning of color at that time and in that place, she made a political choice and entered the door marked "White." Others less self-assured might not. Since that time, there are more colors and continents to choose from as one looks for the appropriate box to check for one's identity. This proliferation in identity possibilities, however, still does not accomodate many Arab-Americans. In her poem, "Browner Shades of White," Laila Halaby evokes the identity crisis of an Arab-American woman who tries to do in the 1990s what El Saadawi did in the 1960s:

> Under *race/ethnic origin*
> I check *white*
> I am not
> a minority
> on their checklists
> and they erase me
> with the red end
> of a number
> two pencil. . . .
> My father is a farmer
> My mother is a teacher.
> I am *white*
> because there is no
> square for *exotic*. . .
> My friend who is black
> calls me a woman of color.
> My mother who is white
> says I am Caucasian.
> My friend who is Hispanic/Mexican-American
> understands my dilemma.
> My country that is a democratic melting pot
> does not. (Kadi 1994)

If identity is predicated on the color of one's skin, then persons unsure about their color will be unsure about their identity. The move from Arab to American to Arab American to Arab-American woman—the hyphen signaling the closer linking of these two identities—and then to woman of color is a postcolonial phenomenon linking Arab women in the United States with crises in the "Old Country." It is marked by four turning points.

The first came in 1948 with the establishment of Israel. Arab immigrants were generally tolerated "and did not attract the widespread hostility directed specifically against Jews, for instance, or before that, against the Irish" (Shakir 1997: 81). After 1948, however, the mandate to become generically American, to forget Arab roots and racialized differences, became more difficult to obey. Each subsequent outbreak of violence pitting Arabs against Israelis renewed the consciousness of American aggression against fellow Arabs, regardless of national specificity. All Arabs in the United States have felt implicated. Each war served as a reminder of their Arabness, moving them away from the singular American identity to the hybridized Arab-American. The Palestinian writer Jean Said Makdisi, who was in the United States during the 1967 war, describes the war as creating "an outburst of cultural hatred, unprecedented in my experience . . . a declaration of war on an entire culture and I was stunned by it" (Shakir 84). The defeat was shocking but also mobilizing. Evelyn Shakir, the author of a study on Arab-American women, comments that this war "galvanized the energy of Arab Americans and stirred them to action" (84). This was as true in literature as it was politics. Palestinian-American critic Lisa Majaj writes that the 1970s "saw the rise of a body of second-generation Arab-American literature, primarily poetry, that engaged and affirmed authenticity, and that paralleled the emergence of a pan-ethnic Arab-American identity bridging the different national and religious identities of immigrants and ethnics of Arabic-speaking background" (Majaj 1999: 68).

The second turning point in Arab-Americans' self-perception came with the Israeli invasion of Lebanon in 1982. Second-generation poet D. H. Melhem described it as a watershed. She had always been drawn to black American poetry because of its affinities with the rhythms of Arab poetry. But until 1982 it had been another's poetry, one she could admire and love but with which she had not fully identified. The Israeli aggression against Lebanon turned her back on her roots, and she found herself emphasizing what was Arab about her Upper West Side Manhattan culture. Ironically, this look inward was accompanied by an outward embrace. Just as she ceased to think of herself as a generic American she began to imagine new connections with minoritarian Americans. The new consciousness of Arabness linked her with the blackness of the poetry she had always loved (Kadi 1994). For others, the Israeli invasion heightened their sense of gender discrimination. In 1983, women who were tired of the unchanging, humiliating stereotypes to which Arab women in the United States were continually subjected founded the Feminist Arab Network (Shakir 1997: 105). Foremost among them were Palestinian women for whom "political and gender-based frustrations have often gotten stirred into the same pot, simmering into a bizarre stew that sometimes braces to action and sometimes simply demoralizes" (127).

The third major conflict in the Middle East to affect Arab-American women's self-perception was the intifada, or 1987–91 Palestinian uprising in the Israeli-occupied territories of the West Bank and Gaza. That this should be the case may be due to the fact that Palestinian women in the Occupied Territories had long been active in the resistance, and may even be considered to be its architects (see cooke 1997: chapter 4). This political activism was well known in the United States. In 1986, the Union of Palestinian Women's Associations (UPWA) founded its U.S. branch in Boston and invited speakers from the region. They found "common ground with progressive Jewish women and 'women of color'. . . . From the beginning, many UPWA leaders have been self-declared feminists, who watch with interest and concern the progress made by their sisters abroad. Like feminists there, they are concerned that women have not achieved leadership positions in the Palestinian political hierarchy, and they are worried by the kind of antifeminist backlash that, a year or so into the *intifada*, pressured women in Gaza into donning the *hijab* (Arabic for veil)" (Shakir 1997: 157).

What Shakir is describing is the emergence of Hamas, an Islamist movement in the West Bank and Gaza, which quickly set itself the task of monitoring women's appearance and behavior as part of its overall strategy of resistance to the Israeli occupation. Because of the visibility of Palestinian women's active roles in the period leading up to the intifada and their subsequent marginalization, their roles and status in the new Palestinian society have become a matter for international concern. The impact of this national experience on Palestinian-American women has been considerable and accounts for the fact that they are the ones more likely to be radicalized along gender and political lines than "third-generation Lebanese and Syrian American feminists" (158).

The Gulf War provided the fourth turning point. It forced a new stage in Arab-American identity formation, particularly for women. Before 1991, few Arab-American women would have accepted the label of "women of color." Yet in the autumn of 1990 and the spring of 1991, as the warmongering and the anti-Arab sentiment increased, so did the sense of persecution among Arab-Americans. It reinscribed the colonial construct that split the formerly colonized Arabs from white Americans, the new colonizers in the Arab world. At the height of the war a radio commentator announced that "there are no hyphenated Americans, just Americans and non-Americans" (Kadi 1994: 82). Whoever was related to the enemy, however distantly, became the enemy. Even when the war was over and the xenophobia directed against Arab-Americans had waned, the sense of otherness and exclusion persisted. Some Arab-American women, such as the girls in the documentary *Banat Chicago*, began to call themselves Arabian. Other women linked their situation with that of other subaltern women in U.S. society and embraced the nomenclature that marked the political connection. They called themselves women of color.

The label "women of color" relocates Arab-American women in the U.S. context. Unlike the melting-pot, race- and gender-neutral U.S. identity Arab women had originally had as a model, this women-of-color identity is a plural, polymorphous, racialized, and gendered way of being a U.S. citizen. This naming process collapses the differences between second-generation Arab-Americans, recent immigrants with little or no English, and people of color. To call oneself a woman of color as an Arab-American woman signifies the desire to become part of a new group, people of color, who contest white hegemony in the United States.

To call oneself a woman of color as an Arab-American woman genders the nostalgia of the singular Arab identity. This nostalgia entails sacred loyalties to an authentic place of origin and to all the people from that place regardless of their behavior. Arab women immigrants to the United States have not been able to criticize men in their own communities or from the "Old Country" without incurring the accusation of cultural betrayal. As symbols and upholders of their cultures, Arab-American women have been expected to be unquestioningly loyal. Loyalty meant "grin and bear it." As women of color, however, Arab-American women live in a different relationship to their country of origin and also to their place of residency. Their self-relocation as Americans places them alongside other minoritarian U.S. women. They are then situated like African-American women, whom Deborah K. King has described as suffering from the "multiple jeopardy" of being neither white women who have a straightforward, single-minded feminist agenda, nor men of color who have a straightforward, single-minded racial agenda, and therefore they fall through the cracks of both movements. Realizing that they have become invisible in contemporary U.S. oppositional politics, they are becoming conscious of the ways in which they are being marginalized. They are developing a multiple consciousness in response to their multiple jeopardy (King 1985). As women of color, Arab-American women are using their newly acquired multiple consciousness to practice a multiple critique. They are learning how to challenge several groups simultaneously so that they can criticize both the United States, their own Arab communities of origin, and any other group to which they may belong in which race, gender, and class intersect to disable women's activism.

To call oneself a woman of color is to embrace and then erase the hyphen between Arab and American that had once provided a precarious bridge over a threatening abyss. As they struggle for a postcolonial, feminist identity in the United States, they braid together several identities with less fear of losing one strand as another briefly takes precedence. When they call themselves women of color, Arab-American women can assume the kind of self-positioning chosen by those who call themselves Islamic feminists. They can begin to imagine new coalitional and oppositional practices that form the basis of a multiple critique. Above all, to band under such a rubric is to demand a new, this time collective, hearing for themselves as for their sisters of color. They throw into question the ways in which Arab and Arab-American women have traditionally been characterized. Arab-American women refigure their identities in new communities that distinguish them from white U.S. feminists with whom they had before associated themselves.

Academic Politics

Nowhere has this realignment of identity been more evident than in the debate about whose voices count in the academic study of Arab Muslim women. Whereas during the decolonization struggles, European and U.S.-based feminist scholars were the first to conduct research on Arab Muslim women, in the late 1980s this situation changed. Foreign white women entered easily into Arab communities, sometimes as adopted daughters, sometimes as wives. From this special vantage point, they compared the Arab Muslim women with themselves. Many declared them victims of an especially virulent variety of patriarchy. Then a new generation of Asian and African women began to study in the United States. In her influential 1988 essay "Under Western Eyes: Feminist Scholarship and Colonial Discourses," the South Asian cultural critic Chandra Mohanty exposed the neo-orientalism and cultural imperialism of western liberal feminist approaches to the experiences of women in Asia and Africa. No, she declared, echoing semantic transformations happening in U.S. feminisms, these women were not uniformly *victims*, they were highly differentiated *survivors*, and those best suited to study them were women who came from the place of study (Mohanty 1988).

In the fall of 1988, the same year that Mohanty published her essay and a few months after the outbreak of the intifada, the then recently formed Association for Middle Eastern Women's Studies (AMEWS) met during the annual convention of the Middle East Studies Association. A panel had been organized to celebrate twenty years of U.S. women's research about women in the Middle East. While several Arab-American women scholars recognized contributions by white U.S. women to knowledge about Arab women, they suggested that it was time to move on. Arab and Arab-American women were poised to bring their different perspectives to bear. They launched a debate that was to continue for over ten years: Who has the right and authority to speak for whom?

During 1988 also, anthropologists Soraya Altorki and Camilla Fawzi El-Solh edited a volume of essays by Arab and Arab-American women anthropologists, entitled *Arab Women in the Field: Studying Your Own Society*. Its contributors addressed what they considered to be problems in non-Arab Western women's approaches to the study of Arab women, such as white privilege. White women enjoyed greater "flexibility and mobility . . . than would be possible for local women." This privilege entailed a handicap, however, because easy access to both men's and women's communities skewed their experience and perception of reality. How could these white women understand life in a sex-segregated society? The editors contrasted these observers flitting easily across usually impermeable borders with women researchers born in the Arab world. Arab women enjoyed few such privileges; they lived as did the women they studied. They understood their experience, and the research they conducted reflected the axiom that to be "part of the same cognitive world implies that subject and object share a similar body of knowledge" (Altorki and El-Solh 1988: 6–7). The editors also claimed that the Arab women researchers were less susceptible to "cultural fatigue" (8). Altorki and El-Solh seemed to be making an essentialist argument about what kinds of people could and could not produce good anthropology of Arab women.

The late 1980s thus marked the beginning of a new stage in the scholarship on Arab Muslim women. It was no longer possible to engage in research and writing without paying attention to the who and where of the production of knowledge. The work of white U.S. women specializing in Arab women's studies was seriously questioned and openly challenged. The challengers were no longer scholars skeptical of the value of the study of women, but rather Arab-American women academics, many of whom had begun their careers in non-Arab fields. Introducing an immigrant Arab imaginary into the study of Arab Muslim women in the U.S. academy, they assumed responsibility for the production of knowledge about Arab, and particularly Arab Muslim, women.

Since the Gulf War there has been a further development. In tandem with the political emergence of a new identity as women of color described above, Arab-American women intellectuals have gone beyond distinguishing themselves from plain Americans to also point out their difference from Arabs. In 1992 Barbara Nimri Aziz and Leila Diab launched the Arab Writers'

Group U.S.A. with its trimesterly newsletter. Within two years, the "Arab" in the title had become "Arab-American" and the group called itself Radius of Arab-American Writers Inc., or RAWI (the Arabic for "Narrator"). In May 1995, when the two-page typewritten memo addressed to "Friends" had become a formal typeset six-page document, the editor lamented the lack of mutuality between Arab and Arab-American intellectuals. Why is it that Arab-Americans love poetry by Arabs but not by Arab-Americans? In the tenth issue, the editor criticized Arab intellectuals for neglecting Arab-American writers. During the Arab Cultural Gala in Chicago in September 1995, the Syrian Nizar Qabbani and the Iraqi Muzzafar Nawwab, two of the Arab world's most renowned dissident poets living in exile, recited their poetry to an audience that had each paid $150 per ticket. Why had Arab-Americans paid so much? Because they wanted "to have something Arab reinforced. That reinforcement is natural and necessary. But I somehow doubt if these same poetry lovers will even know the names of our most accomplished Arab-American poets." The bitterness of this editor is palpable.

The split between Arab and Arab-American women forces an awareness of U.S.-ness, which in turn has given rise to a new consciousness, that of Arab-American *women of color*. They have become the fourth constituency in the field of Arab Muslim women's studies. Arab-American women of color are pointing to the gaps that separate them from Arab, from Arab-American as well as from non-Arab American women. They highlight the coalitional possibilities with each other as also with other U.S. subaltern women. Lisa Majaj exhorts Arab-Americans to go beyond self-assertion to analysis so as "to move beyond cultural preservation toward transformation." This transformation is especially evident in the literary field where "the more rigorous and self-critical explorations mandate a move away from the lyric compression of poetry toward the more expansive and explanatory medium of prose" (Majaj 1999: 71). Political and literary transformation has implications for feminist activism, writes Majaj: "We need a stronger, more nuanced and less defensive articulation of feminism. The enemy is silence, but as long as individual feminists fear community censure they will not dare to explore what is wrong in the society, and what is wrong will not be righted" (73).

Now, over a decade after the dramatic AMEWS meeting revealed the differences between white U.S. and Arab-American women scholars, the field of Arab women's studies has opened up, but not without disruption and new problems. What has changed in the interim is the mandate for self-consciousness and self-reflexivity. The illusion that Arab women are not known and that the scholar engaged in their study is pioneering has given way to a new kind of understanding. Scholars of Arab women are, *nolens volens*, involved in a collaboration, but one that is filled with potential misunderstandings and recriminations. The challenge is to work across very different allegiances and agendas. The point, as Robert Stam writes about scholarship in the multicultural academy, is "not to completely embrace the other perspective, but at least to recognize it, acknowledge it, take it into account, see oneself through it, and even be transformed by it" (1997: 201). The project of examining, rethinking, and redefining oneself as well as the object of study can strengthen those moving in from the margins, even as it threatens others previously located closer to the center of the knowledge-producing industry. The common agenda now is to learn how to talk to each other across our differences, to remain open to each other, welcome encounters with people different from ourselves, and learn to make these differences enriching and creative, while we all learn to conduct a multiple critique. We have to learn to acknowledge and respect differences of cultures, histories, and individual as well as collective needs without silencing each other. For to silence one another is to participate in silencing all those voices we are trying to retrieve and preserve.

Conclusion

Since the end of the cold war, Arab intellectuals have been preoccupied with the problem of how to position themselves in a globalizing universe, but without submitting to and representing the violent politics of extremist religious movements. The Tunisian philosopher Fathi Triki points to the dangers that postcolonial Arabs face as they try to find a niche in the global economy. He warns against the uncontextualized invocation of collective identities, such as Islamism, Arabism,

Nasserism, or Baathism. Without a clear sense of who they are beyond the slogan, these groups may self-destruct. They must learn how to situate themselves in this "new geo-political landscape of a world that remains divided, contested and conflicted." Sloganeering as self-affirmation is "not a way of avoiding transnationalism or of opposing globalization," especially if it happens in what he calls *a dangerous void* (Triki 1998: 14). What is crucial is to speak out, but also to make sure that what was spoken is not later silenced and erased. He warns those who have been frustrated with the unfulfilled promises of development made by local powers and global capitalists not to slip into identitarian politics (18, 47). The challenge is to be free and responsible as individuals and while belonging and submitting to their various communities.

Multiple critique may provide the tactical tools with which to respond to Triki's challenge. Those who want to be free and responsible and yet cultivate inclusion must learn how to position themselves in the religious sphere while acting in the secular, political realm. Balancing their collective and individual identities while interacting with others, Islamic feminists are positioning themselves to play the pivotal role Homi Bhabha has claimed for marginalized groups as they emerge from unexpected places, locate themselves in the world, affirm their identities and thus disturb "the calculation of power and knowledge, producing other spaces of subaltern signification" (Bhabha 1994: 163). This is not an essentialist self-definition based on gender, religion, and race exceptionalism. What I am interested in is how a subalternized group can assume its essentialized representations and use them strategically against those who have ascribed them.

Islamic feminists are not afraid to take on the challenges to their right to seek their own well-being, even when they criticize men and they know that such criticism risks being labeled an antinationalistic or un-Islamic act. Some are taking advantage of the cognitive dissonance in the label Islamic feminist to ally themselves with the Muslim community that protects and upholds women's rights, while at the same time speaking out against patriarchal distortions of the values and norms of the founding *umma*. Others are playing back to the men the strategies they themselves have long used in their anticolonial struggles: make the master accountable for the ethical discourse that his actions contradict. Islamic feminists are studying the same texts that men used to arm themselves. When Western governments tout human rights and universal justice, Muslim men respond by showing Western moral arbiters how they consistently violate their own prescriptions. When Western powers are held at bay, Arab feminists can demonstrate to male authorities that they have done exactly the same, they have violated their own prescriptions about justice for women. Islamic feminists are declaring that, yes, Islam is the ideal just society, but that social justice entails equality for all, including women. Even as they make Islamic authorities accountable for their modernizing, pro-women rhetoric, Islamic feminists confront any who threaten their Islamic or local community, whether they be organizations or individual men, or Christian, Jewish, or secular women. They are demonstrating how cosmopolitan individuals can belong to a number of different communities simultaneously while retaining the rights due them in all spheres, including the right to criticize these same communities. They do so as individual members of various groups, as citizens of their nations as well as of the world, and always as women.

This discourse is emerging at a time when the techno-economic machine that undergirds the Western universalistic project of progress is failing all but the most wealthy. At the same time, alternative worldviews emerging out of the inability or refusal to absorb the values of a positivist westernization seem to be succeeding. This binary of failure and success is not intended to invoke the clash-of-civilizations model, nor to describe a history of decline and emergence from the margins, like Ibn

Khaldun's notions of *asabiya*, or tribal solidarity. Rather, I want to draw a different kind of attention to what is happening in those places where the calculations of globalizing knowledge and power are disturbed. Are those countries where westernization has failed now doomed to global marginalization? Or is there something new happening in those spaces where the nonglobalizable survives? What are the dynamics underlying the construction of new and increasingly effective positionalities, identifications, and networks of accommodation and rejection, creation and endurance? What are the geopolitics of global citizenship for which borders are places across and in which to live, and not lines that demarcate the beginnings and endings of national territories?

In a 1997 essay, the Caribbean-British cultural critic Stuart Hall wrote that

> [the] most profound cultural revolution in this part of the twentieth century has come about as a consequence of the margins coming into representation—in art, in painting, in film, in music, in literature, in the modern arts everywhere, in politics, and in social life generally. . . . Paradoxically, marginality has become a powerful space. . . . New subjects, new genders, new ethnicities, new regions, and new communities—all hitherto excluded as decentered or subaltern —have emerged and have acquired through struggle, sometimes in very marginalized ways, the means to speak for themselves for the first time. And the discourses of power in our society, the discourses of the dominant regimes, have been certainly threatened by this decentered cultural empowerment of the marginal and the local. (1997: 183).

Surely, Hall did not have Islamic feminists in mind when he wrote the above, yet they fit this description of the new actors who are coming into representation from the margins, threatening the discourses of the dominant regimes.

Islamic feminists' critiques of foundational stories are reshaping their self-representations. Their writings demonstrate how new players are networking in those spaces where globalized culture is stopped in its teleological movement, forced to take account of local realities. Those moments of rupture and decentering allow for new configurations of historical Islam and feminism that *disturb the calculations of power and knowledge.* In these women's writings, meanings are not absolute but are constantly constructed anew to allow the speaker to retain control over her speech. Their writings fly in the face of the stubborn image of the passive, oppressed woman. Even as they try to change these images, Islamic feminists are working from within to transform those conditions that justify the persistence of such thinking. Their multiple critique is creating the possibilities for the construction of a society founded on a transformed sense of justice for all.

Works Cited

Abu Lughod, Lila, ed., 1998. *Remaking Women. Feminism and Modernity in the Middle East.* Princeton, N.J.: Princeton University Press.

Afkhami, Mahnaz. 1995. *Faith and Freedom: Women's Human Rights in the Muslim World.* Syracuse, N.Y.: Syracuse University Press.

Ahmed, Leila. 1992. *Women and Gender in Islam.* Yale University Press.

———. 1999. *A Border Passage: From Cairo to America—A Woman's Journey.* New York: Farrar, Straus and Giroux.

Akash, Munir, and Khaled Mattawa, eds., 1999. *Post-Gibran: Anthology of New Arab American Writing.* Syracuse, N.Y.: Syracuse University Press.

Aksoy, Asu, and Kevin Robins. 1992. "Exterminating Angels: Morality, Violence, and Technology in the Gulf War," in Hamid Mowlana, George Gerbner, and Herbert I. Schiller, eds., *Triumph of the Image: The Media's War in the Persian Gulf: A Global Perspective.* Boulder, Colo.: Westview.

Al-Ali Nadje Sadiq. 1997. "Feminism and Contemporary Debates in Egypt," in Chatty and Rabo.

Altorki, Soraya, and Camilla Fawzi El-Solh. 1988. *Arab Women in the Field: Studying Your Own Society.* Syracuse, N.Y.: Syracuse University Press.

Anderson, Benedict. 1998. *The Specter of Comparisons: Nationalism, Southeast Asia and the World.* New York: Verso.

Arberry, A. J. 1966. *Muslim Saints and Mystics.* Chicago: Chicago University Press.

Ask, Karin, and Marit Tjomsland, eds. 1998. *Women and Islamization: Contemporary Dimensions of Discourse on Gender Relations.* Oxford,: Berg.

Badran, Margot. 1991. "Competing Agenda: Feminists, Islam and the State in 19th and 20th Century Egypt," in Deniz Kandiyoti, ed., *Women, Islam, and the State.* Philadelphia: Temple University Press.

―――. 1999. "Unifying Women: Feminist Pasts and Presents in Yemen," in Badran and Miriam Cooke, 1990. *Opening the Gates. A Century of Arab Feminist Writing* London: Virago. Sinha, Guy, and Woollacott.

Badran and Miriam Cooke, 1990. *Opening the Gates. A Century of Arab Feminist Writing.* London: Villago.

Baudrillard, Jean. 1995 (1991). *The Gulf War Did Not Take Place.* Bloomington, Ind.: Indiana University Press.

Bengio, Ofra. 1992. *Saddam Speaks on the Gulf Crisis: A Collection of Documents.* Tel Aviv: Shiloah Institute.

Benjelloun, Tahar. 1998. *Le Racisme Expliqué à ma Fille.* Paris: Seuil.

Bhabha, Homi. 1994. *The Location of Culture.* New York: Routledge.

Bhatia, Bela, Mary Kawar, and Mariam Shahin, eds. 1992. *Unheard Voices: Iraqi Women on War and Sanctions.* London: Change.

Braudel, Fernand. 1995 (1966). *The Mediterranean and the Mediterranean World in the Age of Philip II* (2) Berkeley and Los Angeles: University of California Press.

Brock, Sebastian P., and Susan Ashbrook Harvey. 1987. *Holy Women of the Syrian Orient.* Berkeley and Los Angeles: University of California Press.

Buchanan, Constance H. 1996. *Choosing to Lead: Women and the Crisis of American Values.* Boston: Beacon Press.

Butler, Judith. 1995. "Contingent Foundations: Feminism and the Question of Postmodernism," in Nicholson.

Castells, Manuel. 1996. *The Rise of the Network Society.* Oxford: Blackwell.

―――. 1997. *The Power of Identity.* Oxford: Blackwell.

Chatty, Dawn, and Annika Rabo, eds. 1997. *Organizing Women: Formal and Informal Women's Groups in the Middle East.* Oxford: Berg.

Connolly, Clara, and Pragna Patel. 1997. "Women Who Walk on Water: Working across 'Race' in Women Against Fundamentalism," in Lowe and Lloyd.

Cooke, Miriam. 1988. *War's Other Voices: Women Writers on the Lebanese Civil War.* London and New York: Cambridge University Press.

———. 1997. *Women and the War Story.* Berkeley: California University Press.

Cooke, Miriam, and Angela Woollacott, eds. 1993. *Gendering War Talk.* Princeton, N. J.: Princeton University Press.

Crossette, Barbara. 1998. "Hussein Delivers a New Ultimatum to U.N. Inspectors." *New York Times,* Jan. 18.

al-Dari', Fawziya. 1993. *Al-dars al-awwal. Ru'ya nafsiya li azmat al-thani min aghustus* (The First Lesson: A Psychological Look at the Crisis of the Second of August). Kuwait: Dar Snadal-Sabeh.

Davis, Angela. 1985. "Reflections on the Black Woman's Role in the Community of Slaves," in Guy- Sheftall.

Derrida, Jacques. 1976 (1967). *Of Grammatology.* Baltimore: Johns Hopkins University Press.

———. 1996. *Le Monolinguisme de l'Autre.* Paris: Galilée.

———. 1997. *De l'Hospitalité* (Response to Anne Dufourmantelle). Paris: Calmann-Levy.

Djebar, Assia. 1993 (1985). *Fantasia: An Algerian Cavalcade.* Portsmouth: Heinemann.

———. 1991. *Loin de Medine: Filles d'Ismael.* Paris: Albin Michel.

———. 1992. *A Sister to Scheherezade.* Portsmouth: Heinemann.

———. 1995. *Vaste est la Prison.* Paris: Albin Michel.

Duval, Soroya. 1998. "New Veils and New Voices: Islamist Women's Groups in Egypt," in Ask and Tjomsland.

El Saadawi, Nawal. 1999. *Daughter of Isis.* London: Zed.

———. 1995. "Gender, Islam and Orientalism." *Women: A Cultural Review* 6:1 (Summer).

———.1980. *The Hidden Face of Eve.* Boston: Beacon Press.

———. 1994. *Innocence of the Devil,* Berkeley and Los Angeles: University of California Press.

————. 1986 (1983). *Memoirs from the Women's Prison* London: Women's Press.

————. 1993. "Unveiling the Mind." 1993. Videotaped interview with miriam cooke, Duke University.

Eickelman, Dale, and James Piscatori, eds. 1990. *Muslim Travellers: Pilgrimage, Migration, and the Religious Imagination.* Berkeley and Los Angeles: University of California Press.

Escobar, Arturo. 1999. "Gender, Place and Networks. A Political Ecology of Cyberculture," in Harcourt.

Esposito, John, and Yvonne Haddad, eds. 1998. *Islam, Gender and Social Change.* London: Oxford University Press.

Fanon, Frantz. 1967. *Black Skin, White Masks: The Experiences of a Black Man in a White World.* New York: Grove Press.

Faqir, Fadia. 1991. "Tales of War: Arab Women in the Eye of the Storm," in *The Gulf Between Us: The Gulf War and Beyond.* London: Virago Press.

Farahat, Yasir. 1993. *Al-muwajaha. Nawal al-Saadawi fi qafas al-ittiham* (The Confrontation: Nawal El Saadawi in the Witness Stand). Cairo: Dar al-Rawda.

al-Ghazali, Zaynab. 1986 (1977). *Ayyam min hayati* (Days from My Life). Cairo: Dar al-Shuruq.

————. 1994. *Nazarat fi kitab Allah* (Views on the Book of God). Cairo: Dar al-Shuruq.

Ghossoub, Mai. 1987. "Women in the Arab World." *New Left Review,* Jan./Feb.

Giacaman, Rita, and Penny Johnson. 1989. "Palestinian Women: Building Barricades and Breaking Barriers," in Zachary Lockman and Joel Beinin, eds., *Intifada: The Palestinian Uprising against Israeli Occupation.* Boston: South End Press.

Gilroy, Paul. 1996 (1993). *The Black Atlantic: Modernity and Double Consciousness.* Cambridge, Mass: Harvard University Press.

Giroux, Henry A. 1993. "Beyond the Politics of Innocence: Memory and Pedagogy in the 'Wonderful World of Disney.'" *Socialist Review* 2: 79–107.

Golding, Alan C. 1983. "A History of American Poetry Anthologies," in Robert von Hallberg, ed., *Canons.* Chicago: University of Chicago Press.

Gole, Nilufer. 1996. *The Forbidden Modern: Civilization and Veiling.* Ann Arbor: University of Michigan Press.

Goodwin, Jan. 1995. *The Price of Honor: Muslim Women Lift the Veil of Silence of the Islamic World.* New York: Penguin.

Guy-Sheftall, Beverly, ed. 1985. *Words of Fire: An Anthology of African-American Feminist Thought.* New York: New Press.

Hall, Stuart. 1997. "The Local and the Global," in Anne McClintock, Aamir Mufti, and Ella Shohat, eds., *Dangerous Liaisons: Gender, Nation, and Postcolonial Perspectives.* Minneapolis: University of Minnesota Press.

Harcourt, Wendy, 1999 ed. *Women @ Internet: Creating New Cultures in Cyberspace.* London: Zed.

Harlow, Barbara. 1987. *Resistance Literature.* New York and London: Methuen.

———. 1992. *Barred: Women, Writing, and Political Detention.* Hanover:, N. H. University Press of New England.

Hassun, 'Amir Badr. n.d. *Kitab al-qaswa. Muhawala li ifsad ma tabaqqa min hay-atikum* (The Book of Brutality: An Attempt to Spoil What Is Left of Your Lives). n. p.

Hawley, John S. 1987. *Saints and Virtues.* Berkeley and Los Angeles: University of California Press.

Hazelton, Fran, ed. 1994. *Iraq since the Gulf War: Prospects for Democracy.* London: Zed.

Hélie-Lucas, Marie-Aimée. 1990. "Nationalist Struggle," in Badran and Cooke.

al-Hibri, Azizah. 1982. *Women and Islam, Women's Studies International Forum* 5:2.

Hoffman, Valerie J. 1985. "An Islamic Activist: Zaynab al-Ghazali," in Elizabeth W. Fernea, ed., *Women and the Family in the Middle East: New Voices of Change.* Austin: Unoversity of Texas Press.

———. 1995. "Muslim Fundamentalists: Psychological Profiles," in Marty and Appleby.

Jakobson, Roman. 1990. "Linguistics and Poetics," in *On Language.* Cambridge, Mass.: Harvard University Press.

Kadi, Joanna. 1994. *Food for Our Grandmothers: Writings by Arab-American and Arab-Canadian Feminists.* Boston: South End Press.

Keegan, John. 1976. *The Face of Battle.* New York: Penguin.

Kepel, Gilles. 1985. *The Prophet and the Pharaoh: Muslim Extremism in Egypt* (tr. Jon Rothchild). Berkeley and Los Angeles: University of California Press.

Khatibi, Abdelkebir. 1983. *Maghreb Pluriel.* Paris: Denoel.

———. 1985. "Incipits," in Jalil Bennani et al., eds. *Du Bilinguisme.* Paris: Denoel.

———. 1990 (1983). *Love in Two Languages* (Amour Bilingue). Minneapolis: Minnesota University Press.

Kilpatrick, Hilary. 1991. "Autobiography and Classical Arabic Literature," *Journal of Arabic Literature* 22:1.

King, Deborah K. 1985. "Multiple Jeopardy, Multiple Consciousness: The Context of a Black Feminist Ideology," in Guy-Sheftall.

———. 1999. Les Ombres de Laville. *Pauvres margin aux et minoritaises à Tunis.* Tunis; Manuba Univ. Press.

Lavie, Smadar. 1996. "Blowups in the Borderzones: Third World Israeli Authors' Gropings for Home," in Lavie and Swedenborg.

Lavie, Smader, and Ted Swedenborg. 1996. *Displacement, Diaspora, and Geographies of Identity.* Durham, N.C.: Duke University Press.

Lawrence, Bruce B. 1989. *Defenders of God.* New York: Harper & Row.

Lejeune, Philippe. 1989. *On Autobiography* (tr. Katherine Leary). Minneapolis: University of Minnesota Press.

Lowe, Lisa, and David Lloyd, eds. 1997. *The Politics of Culture in the Shadow of Capital.* Durham, N.C.: Duke University Press.

Macleod, Arlene Elowe. 1991. *Accommodating Protest: Working Women, the New Veiling, and Change in Cairo.* New York: Columbia University Press.

Majaj, Lisa Suhair. 1999. "New Directions in Arab-American Writing at the Century's End," in Akash and Mattawa.

Marty, Martin E., and Scott R. Appleby, eds. 1993. *Fundamentalisms and Society: Reclaiming the Sciences, the Family, and Education.* Chicago: University of Chicago Press.

———. 1995. *Fundamentalisms Observed.* Chicago: University of Chicago Press.

McClintock, Anne. 1995. *Imperial Leather: Race, Gender and Sexuality in the Colonial Contest.* New York: Routledge.

Memmi Albert. 1985 (1957). *Le Portrait du Colonise* (The Colonizer and the Colonized). Paris: Gallinard

———. 1992 (1953). *The Pillar of Salt.* Boston: Beacon Press.

———. 1998. "La Tour de Babel," *Le Figaro,* March 9.

Mernissi, Fatima. 1991 (1987). *The Veil and the Male Elite: A Feminist Interpretation of Women's Rights in Islam* (tr. Mary Jo Lakeland). New York: Addison-Wesley.

———. 1994. *Dreams of Trespass: Tales of a Harem Girlhood.* New York: Addison-Wesley.

———. 1992 (1992). *Islam and Democracy. Fear of the Modern World.* (tr. Mary Jo Lakeland) New York: Addison-Wesley.

———. 1995. "Arab Women's Rights and the Muslim State in the Twenty-first Century: Reflections on Islam as Religion and State," in Afkhami.

Messaoudi, Khalida. 1998 (1995). *Unbowed: An Algerian Woman Confronts Islamic Fundamentalism* (interviews with Elisabeth Schemla). Philadelphia: University of Pennsylvania Press.

Mikha'il, Dunya. 1995. *Yawmiyat mawja kharij al-bahr* (The Journal of a Wave Outside the Sea). Baghdad: Iraqi Ministry of Culture and Information.

Mir-Husseini, Ziba. 1996. "Stretching the Limits: A Feminist Reading of the *Shari'a* in Post-Khomeini Iran" in Mai Yamani, ed., *Feminism and Islam: Legal and Literary Perspectives,* London: Ithaca.

Mitchell, Timothy. 1988. "The Experience of Prison in Islamicist Discourse: The Production of Zaynab al-Ghazzali's *Ayyam min hayati,* unpublished paper, Paris, May–June.

Mohanty, Chandra Talpade. 1988. "Under Western Eyes: Feminist Scholarship and Colonial Discourses," *Feminist Review* 30: 61–88.

Moghadam, Valentine M. 1997. "Women's NGOs in the Middle East and North Africa: Constraints, Opportunities, and Priorities," in Chatty and Rabo.

Moghissi, Haidah. 1999. *Feminism and Islamic Fundamentalism: The Limits of Postmodern Analysis.* London: Zed.

Mokeddem, Malika. 1993. *L'Interdite.* Paris, Grasset & Fasquelle.

an-Na'im, Abdullahi. 1995. "The Dichotomy between Religious and Secular Discourse in Islamic Societies," in Afkhami.

Najmabadi, Afsaneh. 1998. "Feminism in an Islamic Republic: Years of Hardship, Years of Growth," in Esposito and Haddad.

Naseef, Fatima Umar. 1999. *Women in Islam: A Discourse in Rights and Obligations.* Cairo: International Islamic Committee for Woman and Child.

Nasrallah, Emily. 1981. *Al-Iqla aks al-zaman* (Flight Against Time.) Beirut: Nawfal.

———. 1994. *Al-jamr al-ghafi* (Sleeping Embers). Beirut: Nawfal.

———. 1962. *Tuyur Ailul* (September Birds). Beirut: Nawfal. 4th. ed., 1979.

Nicholson, Linda, ed. 1995. *Feminist Contentions: A Philosophical Exchange*. New York: Routledge.

Prochaska, David. 1992. "Disappearing Iraqis," *Public Culture* 4:2 (Spring): 89–92.

Richie, Beth E. 1985. "Battered Black Women: A Challenge for the Black Community," in Guy-Sheftall.

Rifaat, Alifa. 1986. *Distant View of a Minaret*. London: Quartet.

Roald, Anne Sofie. 1998. "Feminist Reinterpretation of Islamic Sources: Muslim Feminist Theology in the Light of the Christian Tradition of Feminist Thought," in Ask and Tjomsland.

Ross, Ellen M. 1991. "Spiritual Experience and Women's Autobiography: The Rhetoric of Selfhood in *The Book of Margery Kempe*," *Journal of the American Academy of Religion* 59:3 (Fall).

Rouse, Shahnaz. 1999. "Feminist Representations: Interrogating Religious Differences," in Sinha et al.

Rugh, Andrea. 1993. "Reshaping Personal Relationships in Egypt," in Marty and Appleby.

Salih, Layla Muhammad. 1983. *Adab al-mar'a fi al-jazira wa al-khalij al-'arabi* (Women's Literature in the Arabian Peninsula and Gulf). n. p.

al-Salim, Warid Badr. (1994). *Infijar dam'a. Al-hayat tahta zilal al-sawarikh* (Explosion of a Tear: Life in the Shadow of Bombs). Baghdad: Dar al-Shu'un al-Thaqafiyya al-'Amma.

al-Samman, Ghada. 1998 (1994). *The Square Moon* (tr. Issa Boullata). Fayetville, Arkansas University Press.

Schimmel, Annemarie. 1982. "Women in Mystical Islam," in al-Hibri.

Scott, James C. 1990. *Domination and the Arts of Resistance: Hidden Transcripts*. New Haven, Conn.: Yale University Press.

Shaheed, Farida. 1995. "Networking for Change: The Role of Women's Groups in Initiating Dialogue on Women's Issues," in Afkhami.

Shakir, Evelyn. 1997. *Bint Arab: Arab and Arab-American Women in the United States*. Westport, Conn.: Praeger.

Shammas, Anton. 1985. *Arabesques*. New York: Penguin.

———.1988. "Hebrew as a Step-mother Tongue. A Palestinian Writing in Hebrew—A Personal Account," lecture at U.C. Berkeley, excerpted in Newsletter IX/2.

al-Sharuni, Yusuf. 1975. *Al-layla al-thaniya ba'da al-alf* (The Night After the 1001 Nights: Selections from Women's Stories in Egypt), Cairo: al-Hay'a al-Misriya al-'Amma lil-Kitab.

Al-Shati', Bint (Aisha Abd al-Rahman). 1967. "Al-mafhum al-islami fi tahrir al-mar'a" (The Islamic Concept of Women's Liberation), lecture at the University of Umm Durman (Sudan), February.

al-Shaykh, Hanan. 1995 (1992). *Beirut Blues*. New York: Doubleday.

———. 1986 (1980). *The Story of Zahra*. London: Quartet.

———. 1989 (1988). *Women of Sand and Myrrh*. New York: Doubleday.

Shohat, Ella, and Robert Stam, eds. 1994. *Unthinking Eurocentrism: Multiculturalism and the Media*. New York: Routledge.

Sinha, Mrinalini, Donna Guy, and Angela Woollacott. eds. 1999. *Feminisms and Internationalism*. Oxford: Blackwell.

Smith, Barbara, and Beverly Smith. 1981. "Across the Kitchen Table: A Sister-to-Sister Dialogue," in Cherrie Moraga and Gloria Anzaldua, eds., *This Bridge Called My Back: Writings by Radical Women of Color*. New York: Kitchen Table Women of Color Press.

Spellberg, Denise. 1994. *Politics, Gender and Early Islam*. New York: Columbia University Press.

Spivak, Gayatri Chakravorty 1997. *In Other Worlds: Essays in Cultural Politics*. New York and London: Methuen.

Stam, Robert. 1997. "Multiculturalism and the Neoconservatives," in Anne McClintock, Aamir Mufti, and Ella Shohat, eds., *Dangerous Liaisons: Gender, Nation and Postcolonial Perspectives*, Minneapolis: Minnesota University Press.

Sternhell, Zeev. 1998. "Une Occasion Manquée," *Le Monde*, March 21.

Taminiaux, Jean Pierre. 1993. "La Guerre du Golfe ou l'histoire d'un monde sans temoin," in *Peuples Mediterranéens*, 64–65.

Tavakoli-Targhi, Mohamed. 1990. "Refashioning Iran: Language and Culture During the Constitutional Revolution." *Iranian Studies* 23: 77–101.

Taylor, Charles. 1994. "The Politics of Recognition," in Amy Gutman, ed., *Multiculturalism*. Princeton, N. J.: Princeton University Press.

Theweleit, Klaus. 1993. "The Bomb's Womb," in Cooke and Woollacott.

Tilley, Maureen. 1991. "The Ascetic Body and the (Un)making of the World of the Martyr," *Journal of the American Academy of Religion* 59:3 (Fall).

Triki, Fathi. 1998. *La Stratégie de l'Identité. Essai.* Paris: Arcanteres.

al-'Uthman, Layla. 1994. *Al-hawajiz al-sawda'* (Black Barricades). Kuwait: al-Qabas al-Tijariya.

Wheeler, Deborah L. 1998. "Global Culture or Culture Clash: New Information Technologies in the Islamic World—A View from Kuwait," *Communication Research* 25:4 (August).

Wilder, Gary. 1996. "Irreconcilable Differences: A Conversation with Albert Memmi," *Transition* 71.

Zayn al-Din, Nazira. 1998a (1928). *Al-sufur wal-hijab* (Unveiling and Veiling). Damascus: Dar al-Mada.

———. 1998/6 (1929). *Al-fatat waal-shuyukh* (The Girl and the Shaykhs). Damascus: Dar al-Mada.

Zeidan, Joseph. 1986. *Masadir al-adab al-nisa'i fi al-'alam al-'arabi al-hadith* (Bibliography of Women's Writings in the Modern Arab World). Riyad. Revised and republished, Beirut: al-Mu'assasa al-'Arabiya li al-Dirasat wa al-Nashr, 1999.

———. 1995. *Arab Women Novelists: The Formative Years and Beyond.* New York: New York University Press.

al-Zibn, Dalal Faysal Su'ud. 1993. *Ayyam al-qahr al-kuwaytiya al-thani min aghustus 1990 hatta 27 fabrayir 1991* (Kuwaiti Days of Oppression August 2, 1990–February 27, 1991). Kuwait: Dar Su'ad al-Sabah.

Zuhur, Sharifa. 1993. "Al-islamiyun fi misr: qira'a fi qadiyat al-mar'a" (Islamists in Egypt: A Reading of the Woman Question), *Qira'at Siyasiya* 3:2 (Spring).

Permissions

The publisher and author are grateful for permission to reprint the following:

Part of chapter 2 appeared previously as "The Other Language and Construction of the Self" in *Peuples Mediterraneens*, 78 (January–March 1997), and is reprinted with the permission of CNRS Editions.

Part of chapter 4 appeared previously as "Zaynab al-Ghazali: Saint or Subversive" in *Die Welt des Islams*, 34 (1994). Copyright © 1994 and permission to reprint by Koninklijke Brill N.V. Leiden, the Netherlands.

Part of chapter 5 appeared previously as "Listen to the Image Speak" in *Cultural Values*, 1:1 (1997). Copyright © 1994 and permission to reprint by Blackwell Publishers Ltd.

Part of chapter 5 appeared previously as "Feminist Transgressions in the Postcolonial Arab World" in *Critique*, 14 (Spring 1999), and is reprinted with the permission of Hamline University Press.

Part of chapter 5 appeared previously as "Multiple Critique: Islamic Feminist Rhetorical Strategies" in *Nepantala: Views From South*, 1 (2000), and is reprinted with the permission of Duke University Press

Index